"Haunting Lusitania"

A Play in Two Acts

Written by

Kevin T. Baldwin

CAST

MALCOLM NEWMAN – American film historian, works with Doug Wells. Handsome man, late twenties to early thirties.

DOUG WELLS – American film historian, Malcolm's associate. Witty, talented. Good looking. Mid twenties to early thirties.

JANICE CONWAY – Irish woman, living in Dover, England. Great granddaughter of and caregiver for Mrs. McShane-Bryce. Early to mid twenties.

ETHEL MCSHANE-BRYCE – Elderly Irish woman, born out of the love of two Lusitania survivors. Lives with Janice Conway in Dover, England.

SCHWIEGER – Mysterious German gambler and tortured soul. RMS Lusitania priest. Weathered looking. Early thirties.

DAVIES – British sailor. Brash, hard working, blue collar type. Can be anywhere between early thirties to early fifties.

FIRST OFFICER ROWLAND – British First Officer serving aboard RMS Lusitania. Rugged looking. Handsome man, late twenties to mid thirties.

CAPTAIN TURNER – British captain of the RMS Lusitania. Late forties to mid fifties.

ERNEST JONES – American filmmaker and producer. Greedy, selfish and lascivious opportunist. Early forties to early fifties.

LILLIAN LUMIET – Former buxom star of early American burlesque stages. Trying to make it big as a silent film actress, in spite of the fact she cannot act. Attractive, brash, selfish and a nymphomaniac. Mid thirties.

YVONNE MCSHANE – Ethel's mother. Irish. Another actress. Jones's assistant. Attractive and down-to-earth. Early to mid twenties. Malcolm's love interest.

ERNEST COWPER – Canadian journalist. Early to mid twenties. Interviews Lillian. Sees the conning tower of the submarine before the torpedo was fired at Lusitania.

ALFRED G. VANDERBILT – American millionaire. Late thirties. Acts like a playboy however is actually a devoted husband who sacrifices his life in the pursuit to save others on board the sinking Lusitania.

RONALD DENYER – Valet for Vanderbilt. American. Devoted servant who also sacrifices his life to save others on board the sinking Lusitania. Late twenties to early thirties.

SARAH LUND – An American woman travelling aboard Lusitania with her husband and father after finding out her mother survived the sinking of the Empress of Ireland.

JOHN WALSH – Handsome British man romantically involved with Gerda Neilson. Proposed to her on the night before Lusitania is struck. Late twenties to early thirties.

GERDA NEILSON – Attractive British woman romantically involved with John Walsh. Proposed to by John on the night before Lusitania is struck. Late twenties to early thirties.

THEODATE POPE - First class passenger traveling with Professor Friend. A middle-aged spinster from a wealthy estate in Farmington, Connecticut. Believes in an afterlife and the power of the mind. Has a slight spiritual quality to her.

PROFESSOR EDWIN FRIEND - First class American passenger traveling with Miss Pope. Mid twenties. Secretary of the New York's Society for Psychic Research. Former professor at a western college but living on the Pope estate with his pregnant wife during the past year.

LADY ALLAN – French Canadian aristocrat with two young troublemaking daughters.

ANNA ALLAN – One of Lady Allan's daughters. French Canadian. Early to mid teens.

GWENDOLYN ALLAN - One of Lady Allan's daughters. French Canadian. Early to mid teens.

DOROTHY BRAITHWAITE – Young French Canadian woman who travels to see her sisters who have both been widowed on the same day. Celebrates her birthday aboard Lusitania.

BARMAID – Verbose, heavyset Irish woman serving in a filthy, guttural Dover bar. Can be anywhere between early forties to early sixties.

MARINER # 1 – Old Welsh fisherman frequenting the filthy, guttural Dover bar. Early forties to sixties.

MARINER # 2 – Old Welsh fisherman frequenting the filthy, guttural Dover bar. Early forties to sixties.

THREE MUSICIANS – Two carry violin cases. All three wear tuxedoes. Flexible casting.

GWYNN JONES – Welsh tenor who performs a song at the Vanderbilt party. Flexible casting.

ONE SAILOR – Drunken. Flexible casting.

FEMALE PASSENGER – Attractive, provocative woman, catches the eye of Ernest Jones. Flexible casting.

SAILORS & FISHERMAN, BAR ROOM PATRONS, VANDERBILT PARTY GUESTS, PASSENGERS - Flexible casting.

The time: 2013

The setting: Dover, England

ACT ONE

Act 1, Scene 1 - Small Bar - Dover, England – Thursday Night

SCHWIEGER – (Slowly emerging from darkness to stage center. He is a frantic, tortured soul. He screams to the sky) Is it enough? How about now? Is it enough? How many more? How many more times? (Waits for a response, then after a beat) Fine. One more, then. One more. (Looks at the audience) The ocean floor is lined with centuries' worth of hulls, wrecks and bodies of doomed ships, sailors and passengers. All those perished souls dying abruptly and violently without a "proper" burial. Now the waters contain their essence. Troubled spirits are fated to spend eternity moving back and forth through time, re-living past sins, foolishly trying to make things right in search of eternal rest. Lusitania knew she floated in dangerous waters, where her predator patiently awaited. It took less than eighteen minutes for her to sink. (LIGHTS DIM on SCHWIEGER as he exits off into the darkness amid the sounds of waves crashing against the shore and a ship's steam whistle off in the distance is heard)

(LIGHTS UP on small bar room in Dover, England. It is a smoky room filled with the sounds of SAILORS AND FISHERMAN from different countries, speaking different languages, yet all laughing and having a good time. DOUG WELLS and JANICE CONWAY enter the bar from a door along the back wall and cross to a table down right. JANICE has a unique film container with special markings in her handbag. TWO OLD MARINERS are seated at the next table. A BARMAID comes up and speaks to DOUG and JANICE)

BARMAID – (Over the noise in the bar, in an Irish accent) What'll ye have, then?

DOUG – (Unable to hear her question, speaks loudly in an American accent) What?

BARMAID – (Much louder) What'll ye have, then? (Shouting to ALL in the bar) Pipe down, ye mutts! (The noise subsides, a little)

DOUG – (After a beat, indicating to JANICE) Janice?

JANICE – (Speaking in an Irish accent) We'll have two waters, please.

BARMAID – Ugh, ye didn't come all the way to Dover for water, didje? We're bloody well covered with it, don't'cha'know. (Laughs)

JANICE – Aye, but me friend here 'n me we're lookin' fer some information, and…

BARMAID – About the White Cliffs? Are ye tourists, then?

JANICE – No, we're just...(Decides not to argue the point) Okay, we'll have two ales, then.

BARMAID – Now ye're talkin' m'language. Two ales, straight up, then. (Exits)

DOUG - I hope you're buyin'. I spent my last dime on the rental car.

BARMAID – Won't the FPRS refund ye?

DOUG – Are you kidding? The Film Preservation and Restoration Society has got more red lines through its budget than you can imagine. I'll be lucky to get them to pay for our plane tickets back to New York. (MALCOLM NEWMAN enters. DOUG sees him) Oh, good, there's Malcolm. (Calling out) Malcolm! Over here! (Sees that every head in the bar just turned towards him in silence. Speaking to ALL in bar) Hi. How are you? Sorry. (ALL bar patrons burst out laughing. DOUG is embarrassed. MALCOLM comes up and sits with DOUG and JANICE)

MALCOLM – Thanks. Couldn't figure out how to park the car.

DOUG – You mean where to park? (Begins munching from a bowl of peanuts)

MALCOLM – No. *How* to park. Damn London rentals are so confusing.

BARMAID – (Returning with two beers) Here ye go. Two ales. (Sees MALCOLM) Ah, I see another has joined ye, then. Another one to tip back, then?

MALCOLM – (Shaking his head) Could I get just some coffee, please?

BARMAID – (Laughs) Another funny one, now. Coffee? Here? We haven't served coffee in over a hundred years.

MALCOLM – Really?

BARMAID – These sailors n' fisherman all come in here t'get blind, pissed drunk, don't'cha'know. Look at 'em all. Not more'n two even speak the same language, comin' from all over. Throwin' darts and playin' pool and havin' a grand ol' time. It wouldn't be a Thursday night if there wasn't at least two or three scraps breakin' out. (Looking at DOUG still helping himself to peanuts) Speakin' a that, lad, ye better be careful. Ye might find a "loosened" tooth in them peanuts ye're eatin'. (Laughs as DOUG quickly pulls his hand out of the bowl) Need a few to look at the menus?

DOUG – We didn't get any menus.

BARMAID – It's written on the table.

DOUG – Really? (Looking at the table, sarcastic) I thought those were limericks. With pricing.

BARMAID – (Hearing a great crash of dishes offstage) Ugh! Ye blasted Turks! Stop playin' darts with them Greeks, then, if yer all gonna act like damned idjits. (Exits)

MALCOLM – Nice gal. (To MALCOLM) Kind of reminds me of your mother, Doug.

DOUG – (Shaking his head) My mother was never that nice.

MALCOLM – What are you going to have?

DOUG – (Still looking at the menu on the table) Diabetes if I eat any of this shit. (Looking up at JANICE) Sorry. 'Scuse my language.

JANICE – That's okay. I want to thank ye gentlemen fer comin'.

DOUG – A find like this really piqued our curiosity, Miss Conway.

JANICE – "Janice", please.

DOUG – (Smiling) Janice. How old did you say the film footage you found was?

JANICE – The canister label was very faded but it looks like it read "May 7, 1915". It was in my great grandmother's closet, tucked away for all that time. (SCHWIEGER emerges from a back room along the back wall, crossing near their table. He wears a non-descript black sailor's cap but wears a nice suit with no tie or ascot) She said she had forgotten about it a long time ago. (SCHWIEGER passes by the table, staring nervously at MALCOLM, then politely tips his hat to JANICE, making his way to a table far up left)

MALCOLM – Uh, you didn't open it, right?

JANICE – Aye. Ye told me not to. I put the canister in a plastic bag, sealed tight, like ye said.

MALCOM – (Rubbing his forehead) Good.

DOUG – (To MALCOLM) Headache still bothering you? (MALCOLM nods) Gonna be okay, Mac? (MALCOLM nods. DOUG takes out a pen and pad) The old lady's (elbowed in the ribs by MALCOLM) the elderly woman's name? What is it again?

JANICE – McShane-Bryce. Ethel McShane-Bryce. She's ninety years-old. (DOUG writes the information down) You'd think she was in her sixties or seventies, though, she's usually so full of life. Lived most of her life with her husband here in Dover. Only recently after his death did she start havin' troubles. I've been her caregiver at her home for the last three years.

MALCOLM – Why not just give the footage to one of the preservation societies here in Europe?

JANICE – As I told you on the phone, she was adamant it had to be given to one Malcolm Newman. Took me weeks to track down just which Malcolm Newman in the states she was talkin' about.

MALCOLM- But how could she even know me? Is she a film buff?

JANICE – (Shaking her head) Last movie she ever saw was "The Sound of Music". Doesn't even own a telly. I had to bring my own flat screen from Dublin so's I could watch "Downton Abbey". She reads books, listens to music, that's all.

DOUG – That's just sick.

MALCOLM – (Admonishing) Doug.

DOUG – Sorry.

MALCOLM – Anyway, I think that is what made us so curious. She said she'd only give it to me in person?

JANICE – Aye. She was…

DOUG – (Interrupting, sarcastic) "Adamant", right. So, we flew thirty-seven hundred miles for what? This film of…well, hell, we don't even know what's on the film. It could be corrupt, (sees something) disintegrated for all we…DUCK!! (ALL THREE duck, hearing another glass crashing against a wall) Oh, those crazy little Turks are at it again. (The three sit back up)

MALCOLM – (To JANICE) How sick is she?

JANICE – Doctor says it'll be a miracle for her t'make it past the week.

BARMAID – (Returns with MALCOLM's beer) Here ye go, mate. Have ye decided what ye'll have, then?

DOUG – (Looks at the table and, again, after a beat) Yeah, I'm still going with diabetes. (Looks up at the waitress) Is there a salad to be found anywhere around here, (Looks at the floor) minus the floor?

BARMAID – Well, the seafood salad's not bad.

DOUG – There's no actual like…seaweed…in it, is there?

BARMAID – (Laughs) Nay. (After a beat) I think.

DOUG – Good enough. I'll have that.

JANICE – I'll have the fish and chips.

MALCOLM – Same here.

BARMAID – Oooh, fancy uppers, have we? All righty, then, be back in a jif, luvs. (Exits)

DOUG - Cool. So, tomorrow we'll meet with this lady…

JANICE – Ethel.

DOUG – Ethel. We'll meet with Ethel tomorrow and then run some vinegar tests on the film.

JANICE – Vinegar?

MALCOLM – We put some small strips of specially treated paper that change color to indicate the severity of degradation. Like a litmus test.

DOUG – Wouldn't take too long. We can head over in the morning from the hotel and work on the film right there in her home.

JANICE – Please, we'd like ye to stay at our home as our guests.

MALCOLM – We don't want to intrude.

DOUG – (To MALCOLM) Are you kidding? Let's save the Society a few bucks, at least. (To JANICE) We'd be delighted. We'll check out of the hotel tomorrow morning and be right over. Oh, by the way, where she kept the film, was it stored in a cool, dry area?

JANICE – This is England, Mr. Wells.

DOUG – I'm going with a "no", then. (To MALCOLM) Conditions aren't great to do this sort of work, Mac.

MALCOLM – I know. (To JANICE, explaining) Films stored under damp, humid conditions greatly accelerates decomposition. (To DOUG) We'll use the equipment we brought with us. (TWO SAILORS fight past the table and the conversation continues) Run the film through your hard drive and see what images can be salvaged. (DOUG looks annoyed) Best we can do. (ONE SAILOR hits their table and drops like a stone to the floor)

DOUG – (To JANICE, smiling) So, Janice, do you come here often?

MALCOLM – (To DOUG) Oh, Doug, did you happen to ask if anyone recognized the canister the film was encased in? Maybe some of these old timers would know.

DOUG – Why? Because they might be film buffs?

MALCOLM – No, because Janice said there was maritime ship markings pictured along the front of the label, indicating it was to be mailed overseas. (Another glass misses their table and crashes) There just wasn't any name to the label.

JANICE – Aye, but I'm startin' to think this bar wasn't the best place to find out.

DOUG – Oh, I don't know about that. Malcolm, where's your phone? You got that picture of the label Janice sent us? (MALCOLM nods) Good. Pull it up. (MALCOLM hands over his phone to DOUG who lifts the ONE SAILOR up off the floor) You. Sprechen sie English? (ONE SAILOR nods) Good. You recognize this label? (ONE SAILOR nods) Excellent. What is it?

ONE SAILOR - Alte Britische marine. (Falls back down below the table. Unseen, is heard throwing up)

DOUG – Wonderful. Thank you. (To MALCOLM and JANICE) Old British Navy. Probably an RMS container. Usually sealed air tight for rough seas. Could have preserved the film. We'll see. (LIGHTS FADE as the sound of the SAILOR throwing up continues. Isolated LIGHTS UP on SCHWIEGER, center, as we hear him speak to the heavens)

SCHWIEGER – (Nervous, trying to contain his obvious emotional turmoil) That one, then? Fine. The old woman. She's the key. (Praying) Let this be the last. Please? (Scene TRANSITIONS to Act 1, Scene 2)

Act 1, Scene 2 – The Home of Ethel McShane-Bryce – Saturday, Two Days Later

(LIGHTS UP on the beautiful home of ETHEL MCSHANE-BRYCE. It is spacious and well furnished. DOUG and MALCOLM are seen sitting at a table center stage working on a machine running film through a projector of sorts and directly uploading the footage onto DOUG's lap top. There is a large flat screen television near the back wall but the entire screen is visible to the audience. There is a beautiful staircase along the back wall towards stage left and a kitchen entrance over on stage right. The entrance door is far stage left. MALCOLM wipes his eyes)

MALCOLM – Holy crap, that vinegar smell is potent. A lot of this is garbage. Images are too decayed.

DOUG – This shit's a century old. High grade corruption all along the sides. Perforations along the grid are brittle. Huh. Sounds like my last date.

MALCOLM – (Smiling, but keeping it business-like) Check the lap top, you perv. What do we have there? (Focusing on the projector)

DOUG – Nothing that wasn't there yesterday. I think we may be done, here, dude. (Goes back to looking at the lap top)

JANICE – (Entering from the top of the stairs) Can I get ye gentlemen anything?

DOUG – (Staring at the lap top) I'm good.

MALCOLM – (At the projector) Thanks anyway.

JANICE – Have ye had any luck?

DOUG – Yes, and although it sounds cliché, it's been all bad.

MALCOLM – I think out of this entire reel we may have salvaged about thirty seconds.

DOUG - How is your great grandmother?

JANICE – (To DOUG) Still unconscious. (To MALCOLM) Since ye arrived she's just been gettin' worse. (DOUG takes another look back at the lap top) I don't think it'll be much longer, now. Doctor said there's nothing to do. Just let her rest.

MALCOLM – I'm sorry we didn't get a chance to meet…

DOUG – (Interrupting) Hey, hey. I think I got something here. (MALCOLM peers over the lap top along with JANICE) It's faint but not oxidized.

MALCOLM – Looks like a silent movie.

DOUG – Not bad, either. Look at that smoke and the fire. Pretty nice work for turn of the century filmmaking and no CGI. Almost looks real.

MALCOLM – What's that along the back wall? Is that a life preserver?

DOUG – Looks like it, but I can't tell what it says.

MALCOLM – Change the aspect ratio, see if you can zoom in on the image then put it onto your flash drive. (Pointing to the television screen, says to JANICE) Your flat screen. Does it have a USB port?

JANICE – Aye, it does.

MALCOLM – Great.

DOUG – (Pulls out the flash drive and hands it off to MALCOLM) Done. If she's got the right port I can just hook up the lap top and run it with the TV screen.

MALCOLM – Great. Let's do it.

(MALCOLM and DOUG hook up the lap top to the flat screen television. SPECIAL EFFECT NOTE: If preferred, the following "images" can be acted out on stage, especially if the technology is not available. MALCOLM starts up the television and we see images of a fire on board a ship. The images are black and white with a brownish tinge to indicate the film has not been re-mastered or restored. It should look very real but very low-tech. There is a smoke-filled cabin. A WOMAN is scared, trapped by the flames. The WOMAN is YVONNE MCSHANE, wearing an elegant party gown. She stops and looks at the camera)

JANICE – My. She's very beautiful.

DOUG – Like a Mary Pickford.

MALCOLM – More like a Louise Brooks.

DOUG – Ooooh.."Beggars of Life". Great flick.

JANICE – I have no idea what ye're talkin' about.

DOUG – (Laughing) Sorry. Old movie actresses.

MALCOLM – (Looking closer at the footage) What's she doing? (THERE is a jolt and the footage skips) What happened?

DOUG – Uh, well, remember if this is an older camera, they had to hand-crank it to keep filming. So, someone might have jumped around the back and filmed whatever happens next.

MALCOLM – She's the most beautiful woman I've ever seen. (After a beat) It's weird. It's like she's looking straight at...(YVONNE mouths the words "Malcolm, please save me! Malcolm help!") What was...wait! Go back. (DOUG rewinds the footage) Doug? Can you tell what she said?

DOUG – I can't quite make it out. Let me try. (The footage repeats itself, only this time, as LILLIAN mouths the words, DOUG speaks them aloud) Holy shit.

MALCOLM – That's what she said?

DOUG – No. She's saying, "Malcolm, please save me. Malcolm help". (Looks at MALCOLM) Wow. The cameraman's got the same name as you. That's really weird.

MALCOLM – (Stunned, realizing) No. It's weirder than that. I believe she…She's calling out to me. (DOUG and JANICE look at MALCOLM) What? I know it sounds crazy, but I swear she is.

DOUG – Dude. That's impossible. This movie is ninety-eight years old. Reminds me of an old animated film I saw in film class once, but as good as the production values are, I've gotta say for a movie…

MALCOLM – It's not a movie, Doug.

DOUG – What do you mean?

MALCOLM - Take a look at the life preserver. (DOUG looks closer at the television, freezes the image)

DOUG – "RMS Lusitania". So…what? Are you saying…? (Dressed in a bathrobe, ETHEL MCSHANE-BRYCE appears at the top of the stairs, unseen by the OTHERS who continue to stare at the television and discuss)

MALCOLM – This is for real. Lusitania was sunk in 1915.

DOUG – I thought that was the Titanic.

MALCOLM – Titanic was 1912, ran into an iceberg. Lusitania was deliberate. They were murdered, sunk by a German sub, torpedoed.

DOUG – A U-boat? Hitler ordered them sunk? That bastard.

MALCOLM – Doug, Hitler wasn't even in the picture in 1915. This was Kaiser Wilhelm.

DOUG – I'm not good at history.

MALCOLM – You're a film historian.

DOUG – I can balance a checkbook, too. Doesn't make me an IRS auditor. German history? I barely know a goose step from goose shit. (MALCOLM and JANICE look at DOUG) What? I only saw the "Producers" once.

MALCOLM – This is incredible. We're looking at the *inside* of the ship. There's raw footage of Lusitania on its side, but nothing of its actual sinking. We're actually inside, on board the ship. (Disconnects the lap top, brings it back to the table and does an internet search) There's a passenger list. I'll go through this to see if I spot any names of filmmakers of the time. Maybe I can find out who she is.

DOUG – An American filmmaker?

MALCOLM – Could be. There were a hundred or so Americans on Lusitania when it got blasted out of the water.

JANICE – Malcolm, do ye really believe she was callin' out to you?

MALCOLM – I can't explain it, Janice, but, yes. Yes…I do. (Points at the lap top screen) There. Ernest Jones. He was on the ship with some of his crew when it went down in 1915. May the 7th.

DOUG – Oh, great. (Laughing) "Juggs" Jones was on board? That's rich.

JANICE - Who is…was he?

DOUG – Minor filmmaker. Mostly did these early nudie films. Tried to do some legit stuff but they all tanked. (JANICE looks at DOUG) What? Film didn't begin with Disney, honey.

MALCOLM - Doug's right. Like all technology that came before it, man's initial reason to watch film was to see…

DOUG – Boobies.

JANICE – (After a beat) Pornography?

MALCOLM and DOUG – Uh-huh.

JANICE – (Disgusted, but understands) That figures. So, if this is Jones's film…

DOUG – Maybe she was one of his models?

MALCOLM – No. No way. Look at her. She's not an actress. She's…

ETHEL – (In an Irish accent, but struggling to get the words out) She's m-my m-m-mother. (Feeling faint)

JANICE – Ethel! (MALCOLM and JANICE rush to the stairs and help ETHEL down and into a seat)

DOUG – I'll get her some water. (Exits off right through the door leading into the kitchen)

JANICE – Gram, are ye all right? (There are various offstage noises coming from the kitchen)

DOUG – (Offstage) Where the hell do you keep the bottled water?

ETHEL – Yes, dear. I'm all right. (Weak as she hears more noises from the kitchen) Ye better hurry before he wrecks the place.

JANICE – Hold on Doug. I'll help. (Exits)

MALCOLM- (Kneels down next to ETHEL) Are you sure…

ETHEL – (Having minor trouble breathing, grabs onto MALCOLM's arm, gently) Not much time, luv. You need…to go back. Go back and save mum. Get her off that boat.

MALCOLM – What? You're tired, Mrs. Bryce…Ethel. Just rest.

ETHEL – I've been resting for weeks, now, lad. I know what I'm talkin' about. Not much time. Must move quickly. Ye told me, years ago. Mom and ye…ye told me…

MALCOLM – Told you what? What did they tell you? (ETHEL just smiles at MALCOLM, who looks back at the television and then at ETHEL) Your mother…what was her name?

ETHEL – Yvonne. Ask her about her favorite tree in Belvoir Forest. (Struggles to keep conscious) But lad, first ye…ye need to find Schwieger.

MALCOLM – Who? Who is he? (ETHEL becomes faint again) Who is Schwieger, Ethel?

ETHEL – Dover. German gambler. In the bar. He is…expecting you. He can get ye back there.

MALCOLM – (To ETHEL) Expecting me? Back where? (Looks at the television and the frozen image of LILLIAN) Back there? (After a beat, realizing) I have to go back there. I have to. (There is more noise from the kitchen)

DOUG – (Offstage) It's the twenty-first century. Who doesn't have bottled water?

JANICE – (Offstage) It needs to be pumped from the well.

DOUG – (Annoyed, offstage) Every time?

ETHEL - (Gently touches MALCOLM's face and smiles) It was good to finally see ye again…after all this time. (Looks at MALCOLM's eyes) I had forgotten. Mother was right. Your eyes are so…so…bright… (Falls unconscious)

MALCOLM – Ethel? Ethel! (LIGHTS DIM. Scene transitions to Act 1, Scene 3)

Act 1, Scene 3 – Small Bar - Dover, England – Sunday morning

(LIGHTS UP on the same small Dover bar from Act 1, Scene 1. It is morning of the next day. Tables are clean and the BARMAID is putting chairs up on the tables as MALCOLM enters)

BARMAID – We're not open yet, luv. Come back at ten.

MALCOLM – Do you remember me? I was here a few days ago.

BARMAID – Ah, yea. The yank. Want some more water, do ye?

MALCOLM – Water? Uh, no, thanks. I'm looking for someone. An old lady told me I might find him here. A German gambler? (The BARMAID loses her smile) His name is…

BARMAID – (Interrupting) And what do ye wanna see 'im for? Stay away from 'im, lad. He's a rough one. Scum he is. A lunatic.

MALCOLM – Is he here? I need to see him. (SCHWIEGER emerges from a back room centered along the back wall. He is nervous but does not want MALCOLM to notice, so he straightens himself up)

BARMAID – Don't take any money from 'im.

MALCOLM – No, I don't need money. I need…

SCHWIEGER – (In a German accent) Time. You need time, Herr Newman. And time I can provide. (Pointing to a chair) Have a seat, would you? (The BARMAID starts to say something to MALCOLM) Leave us, frau. (The BARMAID reluctantly exits. MALCOLM and SCHWIEGER sit at a table down left. SCHWIEGER pulls out a deck of cards and shows MALCOLM. Somewhat nervously asks) Do you play, Herr Newman?

MALCOLM – Some. How does this…?

SCHWIEGER – (Interrupting, pulls out a sharp knife) Please. (Wants to tell MALCOLM something but can't, so instead he says to himself) Fine. (Places the knife down on the table. To MALCOLM) For this gamble you may ask no questions. I, on the other hand, can provide no *answers*. Only the opportunity you seek and the rules to which you will be bound. (Begins shuffling the cards) Aces high?

MALCOLM – Sure, whatever. (After a beat, referring to YVONNE) You know. (SCHWIEGER nods) Then she *was* calling out to me? (SCHWIEGER offers no reaction) Can I save her? Can I save…

SCHWIEGER – (SCHWIEGER nods) You can save her, but there are rules to this game. Strictly enforced.

MALCOLM – It's not a game to me.

SCHWIEGER – *Strictly* enforced. What are you willing to offer in return?

MALCOLM – (Relenting) Whatever it takes.

SCHWIEGER – (Smiles, relieved) Das ist gut. That's what I was hoping to hear. (Splits the deck in half and places one half in front of MALCOLM and the other half in front of himself) Take the top card off of either stack. High card wins.

MALCOLM – What do you get if you win?

SCHWIEGER – (Knowing) You will win.

MALCOLM – (Slams his hand on the deck, adamant) I like knowing the stakes.

SCHWIEGER – (Sits back in his chair, calm) Then leave.

MALCOLM – (Frustrated) Damn it. You know I can't.

SCHWIEGER – (Grim) That's true. That is very true. Neither can I. (Taps the top of the deck) You draw first. (MALCOLM pulls the top card off of his deck)

MALCOLM – (Holding up the card) Ten. (SCHWIEGER pulls the top card from his deck)

SCHWIEGER – Das ist gut. (Holding up the "7" card) Sieben. Congratulations. You win.

MALCOLM – (Rising) What now? Where do I….

SCHWIEGER – (Takes the card and picks up the two halves of the deck) Take off your jacket, please.

MALCOLM – Beg pardon?

SCHWIEGER – (Stern) Your jacket, Herr Newman. (Begins shuffling the cards) Leave it on the table, along with your passport, cell phone, watch, wallet and all your change. You can't take them with you where you are going.

MALCOLM – Will I get them back?

SCHWIEGER – (Stops shuffling, shakes his head slowly, nervously) No. Be clear, your journey is one way. (Resumes shuffling the cards)

MALCOLM - (After putting all his belongings and jacket down on the table) Okay, now what?

SCHWIEGER – (Stops shuffling, puts cards away, then goes to the bar and gets a bottle and a glass) Now you will need to have patience. Be watchful for a man of God. He will also be watchful of you.

MALCOLM – A priest? Why?

SCHWIEGER – (Pours himself a drink) Let us just say "consistency". We prefer it this way.

MALCOLM – Who is w…

SCHWIEGER – (Stern) Again, you ask for answers I cannot provide, Herr Newman. (Takes a drink) You will want to save the ship. You will want to warn the Captain, passengers, crew. Trust me. I know these feelings. I share them. (Pours himself another drink) Your mouth will want to speak the words but your mind will not let you. History will remain the same. It cannot be changed.

MALCOLM – I don't believe that.

SCHWIEGER – No? God, I hope you are right. (Drinks, then pulls money out of MALCOLM's wallet) Go to the end of the pier. Look for the Rätselhaft Ferry. Take the nine o'clock night boat out of Dover heading to Calais. (MALCOLM goes to ask, but SCHWIEGER stops him) You will not need your passport. Give them two hundred pounds. (Hands MALCOLM the money)

MALCOLM – (Taking the money) Two hundred pounds? For a ferry ride? Jesus!

SCHWIEGER – If you do not wish to go…

MALCOLM – No-no. I'll pay. I'll pay.

SCHWIEGER – (Handing MALCOLM a bottle of whiskey) Take this.

MALCOLM – I don't drink.

SCHWIEGER – You will need it. It is a long journey. It will be cold and this will keep you warm. (Puts his hand on MALCOLM's shoulder) Be clear, Herr Newman. You only have but a few hours. Do you understand? (MALCOLM nods) Das ist gut. Be seeing you. (MALCOLM slowly exits the bar, not sure if he can trust SCHWIEGER. Frustrated, SCHWIEGER then takes the knife and plunges it into the table hard. He collapses into his seat again and takes another drink. LIGHTS DIM. In darkness, there is the sound of crashing waves. Scene TRANSITIONS to Act 1, Scene 4)

Act 1, Scene 4 – Ferry – Dover to Calais – Later Same Day

(At LIGHTS UP MALCOLM is seen wandering the deck of the Rätselhaft Ferry. It is a bare stage with only a few deck chairs lining the stage. We hear the sound of the ferry traveling along the water. It is later that evening, almost midnight and MALCOLM is pacing, drinking, cold and very frustrated)

MALCOLM – I must be the biggest sucker there is. I've been sailing on the ocean for hours. (Shouts) Schwieger! (Looks around, complaining) Haven't seen a soul on board the entire time. Nobody on the crew speaks English. I don't even know what the hell kind of language they're speaking. (Looks out into the darkness as a young girl, GWENDOLYN ALLAN, comes on stage right, behind him, appearing to play hopscotch. MALCOLM checks the bottle which is empty now) Empty. As empty as the world. Can't see a thing, not since we left the Cliffs. Damn fog. How long does it take to get to Calais, anyway?

GWENDOLYN – (In SCHWIEGER's voice) Patience, Herr Newman. Patience. (GWENDOLYN runs off)

MALCOLM – What the hell? (MALCOLM chases) Come back here, you little shit! How did you know my name? (Returns) Gone. Damn it. (Sits down in a deck chair that has a blanket on it) "Patience". Patience, my ass. (Covers himself in the blanket and slowly falls asleep as LIGHTS DIM and the sound of the waves get louder. There is overlapping music of a tenor singing "Celeste Aida" from "Aida". Scene transitions to Act 1, Scene 5)

Act 1, Scene 5 – RMS Lusitania – Cargo Hold - May 7th, 1915.

(There is the loud sound of a ships steam whistle. AT LIGHTS UP the ferry set has now been transformed to become the cargo hold of the RMS Lusitania. It is May 7th, 1915 early on a very foggy morning. MALCOLM is on the floor. As MALCOLM wakes up he sees he is bordered by several large crates with the words "munitions" stenciled along their sides. He sits up and sees GWENDOLYN again standing in front of him)

GWENDOLYN – (Speaking now in her own voice, with a French accent. Smiling, curious) Bonjour, Monsieur.

MALCOLM – (Groggy) Wha-what? Hey, it's you.

GWENDOLYN – (Not understanding) Monsieur? American?

MALCOLM – Oui, American. Weren't you German just a…(Looks around) second…ago? Who are you? (GWENDOLYN doesn't answer. She merely shrugs her shoulders and runs away off right)

MALCOLM – Hey! Wait a minute! I won't hurt you. Come back! (MALCOLM rises, but is very groggy. He bumps into FIRST OFFICER ROWLAND and a BRITISH SAILOR, DAVIES, who enter from stage right)

DAVIES – (In British accent) There he is, sir. Just as I said. I was lookin' for Dowie, stokers' mascot.

ROWLAND – (In British accent) You went looking for the bloody ship's cat?

DAVIES – Captain's orders, sir, but I think the daft furball jumped ship night before we left New York. Anyway, I run in here and there he was, what sprawled out on the floor.

ROWLAND – (To MALCOLM) All right. Hop to, man. Sprechen sie English?

MALCOLM – (Groggy) What? Uh, yes, I speak English. I'm from New York.

DAVIES – (Annoyed, sarcastic) Oh, just swell. Another yank.

ROWLAND - What the blazes are you doing here?

MALCOLM – I, uh…where am I? Who are you?

ROWLAND – First Officer, RMS Lusitania. You are in the cargo hold. How did you get here? This is a restricted area. Now, speak up. Come on.

MALCOLM – (In a daze) Not quite sure. There was this little girl, and she was playing hopscotch…

ROWLAND – Good God, man. Have you been drinking?

DAVIES – He has, sir. I can smell it on 'im. Bet he's a stowaway.

ROWLAND – Your powers of deduction astound me, Davies. (To MALCOLM) Well? Are you a stowaway? What is your name, sir?

MALCOLM – No. I paid two hundred pounds. (After a beat) My name is Malcolm Newman and… (Tries to speak about the targeting of the Lusitania but, just as he was told, he is unable to warn them)

DAVIES – (Incredulous) What? Two hundred pounds? For what? Fixin' to be flying strapped to the mizzenmast? (To ROWLAND) He's a looney, he is. Take him to the brig, Mr. Rowland, sir.

MALCOLM – Excuse me, Mr. Rowland, was it? Can you tell me what day it is?

ROWLAND – It's Friday. Friday, May 7th.

MALCOLM – May 7th, 19…15?

DAVIES – Ooh, I was right, sir. He's tipped back a few too many, he has.

ROWLAND – (Looking at MALCOLM's twenty-first century style of shirt and pants) Strangest looking fashion, I must say. Certainly not dressed like any stowaway I've ever seen. All right. We'll let the Captain decide if you should be tossed into the brig. Take him along, Davies. (DAVIES grabs MALCOLM as LIGHTS DIM and the scene TRANSITIONS to Act 1, Scene 6)

Act 1, Scene 6 - RMS Lusitania – Captain's Quarters – Later

(LIGHTS UP on the Captain's quarters. It is moments later. There is a cabin door stage left. CAPTAIN TURNER is seated at his desk stage right. He is arguing with ERNEST JONES, who is wearing the Captain's famous bowler hat)

JONES – So this is why they call you "Bowler Bill" eh, Captain?

CAPTAIN TURNER - (In British accent, grabs the hat off of JONES's head) Give me my damn hat back. I don't ask how you got *your* nickname. (Puts the hat to the side then sits at his desk) Mr. Jones, I do not mind you taking pictures of the crew, images from the deck, or even of the damn fishes. However, I'll thank you to keep the passengers out of your photographic endeavors.

ERNEST JONES – (American accent) Captain. I'm not just taking pictures. I'm filming. (Dramatic) Film, Captain. I'm filming life in this new century. A new century filled with new possibilities, new hopes.

TURNER - Yes, but with the same old enemies, I fear. Now see here, man. There's close to two thousand people on board this blasted floating citadel. I can't be everywhere at once. So I'll ask that you please try to restrict your…your "activities", *especially* when it comes to the female passengers.

JONES – Captain, we were planning to see some remarkable sights today.

TURNER – Yes, and like your Miss Lumiet, I'm sure there are a few *other* women on board who would gladly show you their "remarkable sights" but it won't be on my bloody ship. And speaking of Miss Lumiet, please do keep her curtailed from sunbathing around my bridge crew. I need my men on the lookout for torpedoes…and not bloody *hers*.

JONES – Ah, but Lil is such a fun girl, ain't she? (TURNER is not amused) All right, fine. What about when we get close to the lighthouse at Old Head of Kinsale? Can I take some shots of Lillian using it as backdrop?

TURNER – I don't know why. Quite frankly, after several hundred crossings, once you've seen it as much as I have it's not all that bleeding interesting.

JONES – Funny, I was thinking the same thing about Lil, which is why I wanted to use some of the other passengers. You're not going to stand in the way of great artistry, are you?

TURNER – I'm going to stand in the way of anyone who annoys female passengers by soliciting them to disrobe for naughty pictures.

JONES – Oh, no, Captain. You got it all wrong. (After a beat, dramatic) Film! Remember? Oh, come on! Open your mind to what's going on. I'm tryin' to grow here as a true filmmaker. Silent movies are gonna become more popular than opera.

TURNER - (Chuckling) Can't see that happening. I mean what's the point if you can't hear anything, right? I have a niece who performs…

JONES – I know. Mercedes Desmore. I met her coming aboard. Shame she didn't sail with us, though. (Drawing a curvy outline in the air of a female posterior) Could have gotten some nice shots of her…(Looks at the steely eyed stare of the Captain) of her face, her face.

TURNER– Anyhow, I'll tell you what I told Mercedes which is that I have no use for these "moving pictures". See it as more of a whim, a fad, really. I've seen one or two of them, at nickelodeons and such. Tom Mix. Westerns. Made me laugh. Loved the hats. But I have responsibilities, man. I've no time to spend on such foolishness.

JONES – "Foolishness"? Captain, what about "Quo Vadis"?

TURNER – (Unfamiliar with the name) "Quo" who?

JONES – A remarkable film, two hours long. A visual masterpiece. It's just set a new standard. Just imagine dozens, nay hundreds of such movies being made.

TURNER – (Incredulous) Hundreds of 'em? Each two hours long? Don't be ridiculous! You really expect people to sit through a movie for that amount of time? They'd have to be out of their bleedin' minds. They'd become fat and lazy, just frittering their lives away on meaningless tripe. (ROWLAND enters with DAVIES leading in MALCOLM) Don't we bleedin' knock anymore, Rowland?

ROWLAND – Sorry for the intrusion, sir, but we have a bit of a situation here, I'm afraid.

DAVIES - Found this man in the cargo hold. The…restricted area, sir.

TURNER – (To JONES) Excuse me a moment, Mr. Jones. Your picturesque proclivities will have to wait. (To ROWLAND) Lord, I haven't the time or patience for these continued shenanigans by the passengers on this ship. (To DAVIES) And has anyone found the damn cat yet?

ROWLAND and DAVIES – (Simultaneous, but staggered) No, no sir. Not yet. We're looking. She may have jumped, sir.

TURNER – Blast. And as for this man, Rowland, just put him in the brig with the other three German stowaways.

ROWLAND – That's just it, sir. He's American. Not German. Says his name is Newman.

TURNER – An American? In the cargo hold? Where'd he come from, then?

MALCOLM – (Recognizing JONES) Jones? Ernest Jones? The porn…uh…movie director?

JONES – (Curious as to how MALCOLM knows him) Yeah. That's me. Do I owe you money or something?

MALCOLM – I (struggling to get the words out, comes up with) I remember seeing your name doing some research. So, it was you on the Lusitania.

JONES – What do you mean "was"? I'm still here, ain't I?

MALCOLM – No, I mean yes, sir. Sorry. I'm just a big fan…of your…work. Name is Malcolm.

JONES – "Fan"? A big "fan" did you say? I don't know what that is. Is that good?

MALCOLM – Yes, sir. (To TURNER) Look, Captain, I paid before I got on. I swear.

DAVIS – Claims he paid two hundred pounds.

TURNER – Two hundred pounds?

ROWLAND – Could be, sir. Seems several passengers paid passage to the purser just as they boarded. Which explains why their names weren't on our initial passengers list

TURNER – Damnable way to run a cruise line. Well, at least we have toilets. (To JONES) Mr. Jones, is this man one of your film lot, then?

JONES – (Looking at MALCOLM, then) Yeah, he's part of my crew. You can let him go, Rowland.

ROWLAND – (To DAVIES) Let him go. (To MALCOLM) Sorry, Mr. Newman, but we've got to be careful in these waters. There are eyes everywhere.

JONES – (Making a billboard marquis with his hands) "Spies and Eyes". Hey, I like that title. C'mon, Newman, let's get outta here. (To TURNER) Captain, I promise my crew won't bother the passengers any further.

TURNER - And proper behavior around the ladies, please. I don't want any more complaints.

JONES – Of course, Captain. We'll be absolute gentlemen or my name ain't "Juggs" Jones. Regards to your niece…and your maid. (Grins at TURNER, who returns a harsh, cold stare to JONES. To MALCOLM) Let's go. (Exits)

ROWLAND – What did he mean by that, sir?

TURNER – (Snapping) Never mind. Damned nuisances, every one of 'em. Between passengers peering out of portholes, leaning over railings, looking for U-boats, lewd behavior by filmmakers transgressing upon our passengers, Vanderbilt throwing wild parties in his cabin, and other passengers pestering me about lifeboat drills… Makes me wish I were captaining a garbage scow. No wonder Captain Dow retired. (ROWLAND laughs) Dismissed. (THEY turn to exit) Wait. (The MEN turn back) Rowland, I want you to see to it that the portholes are sealed.

ROWLAND – Its heavy fog out there right now sir. Coming up on Fastnet soon.

TURNER – But the fog will lift, so seal them all. Blacken them if you have to, but do it now. Passengers are becoming absolute wrecks. Should never have told them about the sightings. Damned gossipy females on staff, getting passengers all worked up, doesn't make our job any easier. Bunch of nervous nellies, if you ask me.

ROWLAND – Can't blame them, sir. Everyone has been on pins and needles since the Germans put that warning notice in the paper.

DAVIES – Aye, an' who does that, anyways? Who writes an ad, sends it to the papers, sayin' "ooh, ye better watch out. Better not take this trip. Ye might be bashed, don't'cha'know". (Looks at ROWLAND and the CAPTAIN) I'm just sayin'. (Realizes he hasn't been given permission to speak, returns to attention) Sorry, sir.

TURNER – Dismissed.

DAVIES – Right you are, sir. (Salutes then exits. CAPTAIN and ROWLAND burst out laughing)

ROWLAND – Sorry about that, Captain. He's a good man, though.

TURNER – No, no. I agree. Davies actually makes a good point, though. Of course, it certainly didn't help matters when we had to wait in Glasgow for those forty or so passengers from the Cameronia.

ROWLAND – Aye, sir. If we didn't have that two hour delay we might not now even be looking for submarines.

TURNER – Right. Make sure the bridge continues top speed and double the watch for U-boat sightings through these waters.

ROWLAND – (Nodding) Fast as we can go on three, sir. Short one boiler, remember.

TURNER – (Sighs) Damn unreasonable this war. How can I run a proper ship on only three boilers? Tell Chief Engineer Bryce best speed as he can, then, steady as she goes.

ROWLAND – Aye, sir. (After a beat) Oh, but we had another directive about zigzagging patterns, sir.

TURNER – (Shaking his head) Steady as she goes, Rowland. Four point bearing.

ROWLAND – But, sir…

TURNER – Rowland, after Titanic sank, I testified to offer my professional insight. They asked me, as a captain of a similar size and scale ship, if anything could be learned from the Titanic sinking. I told them "No". Do you know why?

ROWLAND – No, sir.

TURNER - You can only prepare so much, Rowland. We are in a damned war zone. If we zigzag before a U-boat even sees us, what bloody good will that do us, then? If they want to fire upon us, time is on their side. Moving or not, they'll fire upon us the moment they get a good shot aligned.

ROWLAND – And our "cargo", sir?

TURNER – (Cautious in his response) These are perilous times, Rowland, and unless we are vigilant disasters like Titanic will happen again. (After a beat) Steady as she goes, First Officer, but keep the crew on alert. (ROWLAND turns to go) And Rowland? (ROWLAND turns back again) Keep those damnable passengers away from me for the duration. I'm going to write a letter to my "maid" then I'll be out on the bridge within the hour. Understood?

ROWLAND – To your...(TURNER looks at ROWLAND. Rowland realizing) Ah, yes, sir. (Salutes) Aye, Captain. (Exits)

TURNER – (Takes out a pen and paper and begins writing, saying out loud) My dearest Mabel...

(LIGHTS DIM. Scene TRANSITIONS to Act 1, Scene 7)

Act 1, Scene 7 – RMS Lusitania - Ernest Jones Cabin – Moments Later

(LIGHTS UP on a second class cabin room. There are two bunk beds center stage with a door on either side. The stage left door leads into a bathroom and the stage right door is the entrance door. There are various luggage and storage lockers cluttering the room. It is a claustrophobic space. Actress LILLIAN LUMIET is drinking wine while having her toenails painted by young YVONNE MCSHANE. LILLIAN is listening to music and a loud party going on above them)

LILLIAN – (In a thick Chicago accent) My God! Just listen to that! Sounds like they're havin' a hot time at Vanderbilt's party.

YVONNE – (In an Irish accent) It's seven o'clock in the morning and they have been drinking and makin' noise all night.

LILLIAN – I know, and I already missed *most* of the fun shootin' this damn movie. I don't wanna miss out on any morning rushes, if you know what I mean.

YVONNE – I'm sorry. I don't.

LILLIAN - I means I'm gonna go through my lockers to find a nice slinky dress to wear for Mr. V upstairs. He's supposed to be a real big spender and I am definitely gonna get me some of that. Hurry up with those toes, girly. Let's get to the party.

YVONNE –I'm goin' as fast as I can, Miss Lumiet.

LILLIAN – I know, I know. (Filing her nails, gossiping with YVONNE) So, I overheard the Bartletts talking? Turns out they're headin' back to London after visitin' with Mrs. Bartlett's sister in Chicago.

YVONNE – That's where you're from, isn't it?

LILLIAN – Hell yeah. So, it turns out her brother-in-law is this handsome shyster Alfred Platt, of the Chicago firm of "Mayer, Meyer, Austrian and Platt"? (Licking her lips) Oooh...I wanna meet him.

YVONNE –But, ye said he's married.

LILLIAN – (Annoyed) So what? So were my first three husbands. That's what's so great about 'em, girly. They've already been "housebroken" so I don't have to deal with any of that shit. I just scoop 'em up and when I'm done with them, drop 'em like a hot potato, takin' 'em for all they got.

YVONNE – And these men fall for it?

LILLIAN – (Boasting) Every single time, honey.

YVONNE – What?

LILLIAN – Sure. It's easy. (Demonstrating) I just smile, bat my eyes, squeeze some cleavage and boom! I become the next ex-Mrs. Mayer, Meyer, Austrian and Platt. (Looks as if a light bulb just went off above her head) Hey, forget him! I just remembered! Vanderbilt had an affair on a railway car and the lady committed suicide.

YVONNE – (Blessing herself) How horrible!

LILLIAN - How expensive. Honey, it cost him ten million in his divorce. I heard he paid this guy Williamson to cover the whole thing up for him. He re-married, like a putz, but I can take care of that. Mrs. Lillian Vanderbilt! (Licking her lips) Ooh, yeah. I like the sound of that. (Winces in pain) Ow! You nicked me, you little Irish bitch! Watch it.

YVONNE – (Stops) Sorry, but ye keep movin'...and squeezin'. (Resumes painting LILLIAN's toenails, desperately trying to change the subject) Didje see Lady Anna's daughter Gwendolyn playin' hopscotch on the upper deck? (LILLIAN looks more annoyed) She and her sister are such adorable younguns. Reminds me of when I was a child. There was this tree and we used to climb...

LILLIAN – (Grabbing another drink, interrupting) Sorry, hon, but I don't "do" children. They take way too much of a man's attention away from taking care of the more important things in life...like me. (There is a knock at the cabin. Reporter ERNEST COWPER is on the other side)

ERNEST COWPER – (From behind the door) Everybody decent?

LILLIAN – Lord, I hope not. Come in!

COWPER – (Entering from stage right) Good morning, ladies. Can either one of you tell me where I might find Lillian Lumiet?

LILLIAN – (Looking at her body and then up at COWPER) Well, I see my fame does not precede me.

COWPER – Oh, my apologies, Miss Lumiet. I'm Ernest Cowper. I'm a reporter from Canada. (After a beat) I haven't seen any of your films.

LILLIAN – Your loss. (Looking at him curiously) Then just what the hell do you want there, kid?

COWPER – Well, my editor, Percy Rogers, eh, is on board with me and he has seen your films...all three of them, in fact...and he sent me down to get an interview with you.

LILLIAN – Oh, did he now?

COWPER – Yeah, he said to me as long as they don't invent sound pictures you could be the biggest star ever to hit the theatres.

LILLIAN – Hey! Now, we're talkin'. (Joking to YVONNE) No pun intended.

COWPER – Sure. He said you could probably be even bigger than Lillian Gish.

LILLIAN –Lillian Gish? Gimme a break. She was just lucky Griffith found her for "Birth of a Nation". Me? I'm one hundred percent an original.

YVONNE – (Stops painting) I'm sorry, but isn't yer real name Gertrude?

LILLIAN – Keep paintin', sister. Keep paintin'. (YVONNE returns to painting LILLIAN's toenails) Look, kid. I'm heading out to the Vanderbilt party soon, so we gotta make this snappy.

YVONNE – (Stops painting) Done.

LILLIAN – Good. (Looks at them) Well, it'll have to do. (To COWPER) How long, kid?

COWPER – Oh, it'll only take about twenty minutes.

LILLIAN – (Rising) Twenty minutes? Kid, the "Empress of Ireland" went down in under twenty minutes...although I never knew her personally (Laughs, but neither COWPER nor YVONNE laugh). What? Too soon? Forget it. I got a party to get to. Kid, grab me a dress outta my trunk. Take one for yourself, as well.

YVONNE – (Embarrassed) Oh, no. I couldn't. I'm no good at parties.

LILLIAN – That's because you haven't met the right guy, yet, honey. Just stick with me. Go ahead. Pick out a dress. (YVONNE picks out a dress from the trunk but LILLIAN grabs it away from her and throws it back in) Not that one! That's the outfit I wear goin' to confession on the weekends. (To COWPER, winking) I wear it a lot. (Begins to disrobe, stunning COWPER. She wears appropriate lingerie of the period) Whoa! I guess you really *haven't* seen any of my pictures. (Laughs) What's wrong, kid? Ain't you ever seen a dame before? (Leaning toward COWPER) You're not a virgin, are you?

YVONNE – (Shocked) Miss Lumiet. (LILLIAN laughs again)

COWPER – (Very uncomfortable, turns his back to her) Miss, Lumiet. W-Why don't I meet you up at Mr. Vanderbilt's and we can discuss this more there?

YVONNE – Sure. I'll be up there in a few. (COWPER begins to go) Hey, kid! (COWPER turns back and LILLIAN flashes him quickly, squeezing her cleavage and batting her eyes. COWPER runs out of the room as LILLIAN laughs. JONES and MALCOLM enter the cabin, JONES looking at where COWPER exited)

JONES – Who was that? (Sees LILLIAN) Lil. Cover up, you whore.

LILLIAN – I ain't a whore. I may be a fun girl, but I ain't obscene.

JONES – I write your checks. You're obscene. (Goes into the bathroom and comes out with an old style hand cranked camera on a tripod) Here we go. Lil. I wish you'd stop leaving this thing in the bathroom. What do you do with it in there? (LILLIAN starts to answer) Never mind. I don't want to know.

LILLIAN - (Sees MALCOLM and immediately throws a flirty grin his way) Oooh. Who's this?

JONES – Lil, this is our new cameraman, Malcolm.

MALCOLM – Pleased to meet you. (Sees YVONNE) It's you. (YVONNE smiles at MALCOLM but then quickly looks away, shy)

LILLIAN – (Thinking MALCOLM is talking to her) Yeah, it's me. Me in all my glory. (Begins to get dressed. Says to YVONNE) Help me pick something, kid. (To JONES and MALCOLM) Where's Doug?

MALCOLM – Well I left him at...(realizing she doesn't mean his friend, DOUG) umm, what?

LILLIAN – Doug? The cameraman?

JONES – (Setting up the camera and tripod) He's upstairs passed out in Vanderbilt's tub. It's nothing but one big orgy up there. (LILLIAN looks at JONES deadpan for half a beat before grabbing up the rest of her clothes and the rest of her bottle of wine and running out the door)

LILLIAN – (Rushing) 'Scuse me. (Exits)

JONES – Okay. So, you ever work a camera like this before?

MALCOLM – Uh, sure. (Gets behind the camera. Plays with it a moment and starts cranking it. Sees YVONNE and asks) Say, Yvonne. Can you smile or say something? Do something for the camera?

YVONNE – (Begins to smile, then realizes) How did ye know my name?

MALCOLM – (Evasive) Uh, I guess Jones told me up in the Captain's quarters.

JONES – I did? Jeez, I don't remember. Man, my memory's fadin'. So, Yvonne, give Malcolm a little smile for the camera.

YVONNE – (Hesitant) Oh, no.

JONES – Come on. (Pulling up his own pant leg, demonstrating) Maybe show a little leg or something. Give the guy a thrill. Know what I mean, baby? Shake what the good Lord gave ya.

MALCOLM – Mr. Jones, I...

YVONNE – (Embarrassed) Oh, no. Oh, goodness, no. (Runs into the bathroom and shuts the door)

JONES – (Disappointed, looking in the direction she exited) Yeah, that's about what I'd expect. (To MALCOLM) You have to forgive Yvonne. I hired her on my last trip to Belfast. She makes a great assistant, but I swear she just ain't never gonna do anything of value on the screen. Lord knows, buddy, I've tried.

MALCOLM – Well, I guess it has to be under the right circumstances.

JONES – (Heading toward the cabin exit) Come on. I wanna get some footage of the party. (MALCOLM stares off at where YVONNE exited as MALCOLM picks up an old style suit coat and throws it at MALCOLM) Here. You must have been freezing in that cargo hold. Of all the places to stow away. (Shrugging shoulders, MALCOLM puts on the suit coat but stares back at the bathroom, wanting to approach and speak with YVONNE) Well, come on. Take the camera, unless you wanna learn how to speak German with those guys in the brig. (MALCOLM relents and grabs the camera and tripod)

MALCOLM – Who were those Germans they were talking about, anyway? Spies? Was one of them named Schwieger, by chance?

JONES – Nah, those schmucks were just part of my crew. They got a little rowdy last night and Rowland had them hauled off. (Bangs on the bathroom door and shouts to YVONNE) Yvonne! We're going upstairs to Vanderbilt's. Put on a fancy dress, then come join the party. Maybe you'll meet the man of your dreams there. (Laughs, then says to MALCOLM) Come on, buddy. Let's go. (They exit, closing the cabin door behind them. YVONNE returns into the cabin and looks longingly at where MALCOLM has exited. She opens up LILLIAN's trunk and grabs LILLIAN's "confession dress" as LIGHTS DIM. Scene TRANSITIONS to Act 1, Scene 8)

Act 1, Scene 8 - RMS Lusitania - Vanderbilt Parlor Suite – Moments Later

(Beginning in darkness GWYNN JONES is heard performing the end of the magnificent tenor aria "Celeste Aida" from "Aida". He is accompanied by FIVE MUSICIANS. He finishes as LIGHTS UP on the Vanderbilt parlor suite. It is a short time later. The room is elegantly furniture and filled with happy, inebriated VANDERBILT PARTY GUESTS who applaud when the tenor bows and exits the room with the MUSICIANS. The GUESTS have obviously been partying all evening and into the early morning hours. At the end of the song LILLIAN enters from stage left, wearing a fox tail and being chased into and around the room by millionaire ALFRED G. VANDERBILT. He has also been drinking and wields an unloaded rifle while LILLIAN is acting like a fox on the run. The GUESTS see the rifle and hurriedly exit. LILLIAN hides behind the sofa center)

VANDERBILT – Come along, my little fox. (LILLIAN pops her head out at VANDERBILT. She has a "deer-caught-in-the-headlights" expression. He sees her, aims then clicks the gun. She cries. The gun merely clicks) Bang-bang. (Laughs)

LILLIAN – You missed me, hon. (She leaps onto VANDERBILT, thrusting him down onto the couch, both howling with laughter. She climbs on top of him and he spins her onto the ground) Hey! What gives?

VANDERBILT – Sorry, my aggressive little fox, but I'm afraid my wife might walk in.

LILLIAN – (Starts to climb up onto the couch and rolls back on top of VANDERBILT) Isn't she in New York?

VANDERBILT – True, true.

LILLIAN – Then…lay on, MacDuff! (Hops up and down on his stomach, screaming) Yahoo! Ride 'em, cowboy! Yee-hawww!

VANDERBILT – (More annoyed than turned on) Aren't you supposed to be in SILENT films?

LILLIAN - (Stops "galloping" suddenly, turning pale in expression) I think I'm gonna throw up.

VANDERBILT – (Panicking) Denyer! Denyer! (VANDERBILT's valet, DENYER, enters hurriedly from offstage left, crosses up to VANDERBILT and removes the ever clinging LILLIAN from his chest)

LILLIAN – Oh, good. The more the merrier! (LILLIAN passes out in DENYER's arms)

DENYER – What shall I do with her, sir?

VANDERBILT – (Taking a drink) Not sure. Maybe I should have succumbed to her…charms, for who knows? Soon we could all be dead.

DENYER – Oh, Mr. Vanderbilt, sir. Think of it. You wouldn't want to be caught dead in the arms of a (LILLIAN hiccups in his arms) woman like this, now would you?

VANDERBILT – That's the way many will imagine me going, I'm afraid, Denyer. The rich playboy always engaged in sexual escapades. They don't want to think of me dying like a good man. Strange, isn't it? You and I, we missed dying on the Titanic. Now we may get snuffed by a damned U-boat.

DENYER – (Gently placing LILLIAN on the couch) Come now, Mr. Vanderbilt. You told the papers it was nothing but a hoax, an idle German threat.

VANDERBILT – You know as well as I that what I said to the press was only to keep people from panicking and to save face. If we sink I won't be remembered as a coward. I only wish I had learned to swim.

DENYER – But, there's no reason to think…

VANDERBILT – Oh, look at the writing on the wall, man. The newspaper warnings. The Captain admitting to us last night that there is a submarine out there, stalking us like a predator. I'm used to being the hunter, not the prey. Why do you think I wanted this party? I wanted people to forget. (Admitting) Very well, I wanted to forget. But now, its dawn and time may be running out. (After a beat, looking at YVONNE who is giggling in her stupor) Take her into my state room for now. Let her sleep it off.

DENYER – Very well, sir. (Picks LILLIAN up off the couch and thrusts her over his shoulders, exiting the party stage left. SARAH LUND approaches VANDERBILT)

SARAH LUND – (In an American accent) Mr. Vanderbilt, sir.

VANDERBILT – Ah, Mrs. Lund.

LUND – Wonderful party. But that woman I just saw you with…

VANDERBILT – Just a friend, Mrs. Lund, just a friend. She was, uh, reminding me of just how much I miss my…horses…back home. Where are your father and husband?

LUND – Charles and my dad are off playing shuffle board on deck with some of the others. We just wanted to say we were glad to have met you and we hope to see you again once we're back in New York.

VANDERBILT – I hope so, too. I just hope there is good news for you in Liverpool.

LUND – Oh, well, at least we know mother didn't perish aboard the Empress, after all.

VANDERBILT – But to find out she's in a sanitarium…

LUND – But she's alive, and father is happy knowing that she is being taken care of. For almost a year, he thought her lost for good. He felt he never had a chance to say goodbye. (Smiling) Now he will see her, be with her again, and his mind will be at ease from that.

VANDERBILT – You have a wonderful way of looking at things, Mrs. Lund. I do hope Charles realizes what a lucky man he is.

LUND - I better be getting back to shuffleboard. I know my Charles will be looking for me. (She turns to leave, VANDERBILT gently reaches out to her)

VANDERBILT – Mrs. Lund, you make me...

LUND – What, sir?

VANDERBILT – (Gently, smiling) You make me miss *my* wife, Mrs. Lund. Do be well. (LUND smiles and exits. DENYER returns and crosses to VANDERBILT)

DENYER – They want you back at the poker game, sir.

VANDERBILT – Sorenson's still at it, eh, Denyer?

DENYER – Of course. Even should we get struck by Germans, sir, I do believe he won't relinquish his cards until he knows for certain that he has a losing hand.

VANDERBILT – (Laughs, then asks) Is he still playing with Mr. Williamson?

DENYER – No, sir. Mr. Williamson took off with Miss Baker.

VANDERBILT – (Taking out a cigarette and lighting it up) Williamson better watch out or that beautiful chanteuse might just make an honest man of him.

DENYER – Too little too late, if you ask me, sir. How much did he want from you this time?

VANDERBILT – Enough for it to sting a bit. The strange thing of it is, Denyer, Williamson has "taken care" of some issues for me in the past...I felt I owed him. Little did he know I probably would have helped him anyway. He didn't need to blackmail me. Now, he can scamper off all he wants. I hope I never see his disreputable face again, the bastard. (Laughing) Come along, then. (VANDERBILT and DENYER exit. MALCOLM and JONES enter from stage left, looking around at the party)

JONES – Okay. Set up here. (MALCOLM sets up the tripod)

MALCOLM – Just start cranking?

JONES - Yeah. Oh, get a shot of these two. Maybe they'll start sucking face or something. (MALCOLM and JONES move stealth fully out of the way so the following couple doesn't realize they're being filmed. JOHN WALSH and GERDA NEILSON enter from stage right and cross to center next to the couch. GERDA looks at a beautiful diamond ring on her finger)

GERDA – (In a Swedish accent) This cannot be happening. I can't stop looking at it, John. It is too much. The diamond is so gigantic. In Heaven's name, where did you get this?

JOHN – (Laughs, then says in an American accent) Would you believe I got it from a priest in a poker game? (She laughs) No. We did play last night but during the game he just handed it over to me. Just like that. I asked him where he got it. Said he was to give it to someone he knew was in love. It was like he knew I was going to propose. Must have gotten it from one of his parishioners or something.

GERDA – (Horrified) I can't take the ring of some strange dead woman.

JOHN – Relax, darling. The priest assured me. He said the ring was "meant to be yours". (GERDA relents, smiling and nodding) Oh, darling, you've made me the happiest man on earth.

GERDA – (Sits down on the couch) My head is spinning. We are moving so quickly. We just met days ago. There were times in my life where I felt I couldn't take much more. I want nothing more than to make you happy.

JOHN – (Kneels on the floor beside her, taking her hand) I knew from the moment I laid eyes on you that I was in love. No matter what, darling, I'll never leave you. (SHE nods, smiling) Oh, Gerda.

GERDA – Oh, John. (They hug)

JONES – Oh, shit. (To MALCOLM) Well, brother, this sucks. A shipboard romance? How boring. I'm looking for some sex, some excitement.

(JOHN and GERDA exit off right as YVONNE appears far stage right. She has changed into the more elegantly refined "confession dress", the same one she wore when MALCOLM first saw her on camera. She is offered a small drink by a WAITER but pantomimes her polite refusal. SHE walks around, looking at the partygoers. MALCOLM turns and sees YVONNE but she disappears into a CROWD. MALCOLM stops filming and doesn't hear any of the following as JONES continues his rant)

JONES - You know what would be great, though? If these two had like a "Romeo and Juliet" type of thing going. Yeah, where we're on this big ship, and there's this struggle of class against class, and then the ship goes down and…(Realizing) Nah, nobody'd ever buy it. (Notices that MALCOLM has stopped filming) What are you doing? Keep filming. Get these two older people coming. (Disappointed) Oh, wait. Christ. It's the mediums.

MALCOLM – The what?

JONES – Clairvoyants. Couple of real whackos. Mentalist freaks. Just watch. Maybe they'll hold hands and try to contact Lincoln. My luck, though, they'll only get McKinley. (MALCOLM and JONES once again move stealth fully out of the way so the following couple doesn't realize they're being filmed. PROFESSOR EDWIN FRIEND and THEODATE POPE enter from stage right and cross up to the couch. POPE sits on the couch and takes off her shoes)

POPE – I'm out of breath! It's so noisy in here. Oh, I can't dance anymore, Professor. I'm afraid I'm too old for this. I can't believe how much energy you possess, though.

FRIEND – From my years at Princeton, Miss Pope.

POPE – Come. Sit. (FRIEND sits next to her) Weren't those psychic demonstrations in England simply fascinating?

FRIEND – (A little unnerved) Yes, absolutely. I took substantial notes on everything we learned.

JONES – (To MALCOLM) This is so boring I think I'm gonna puke.

POPE – I can't wait till we get home. I'm sure we'll learn so much from the data you collected. And think of how much it would help the war effort back home to know of attacks in advance.

FRIEND – (Distracted) Yes…yes, quite.

POPE – You miss Marjorie, Professor?

FRIEND –Yes. I'm worried.

POPE – You needn't be. I'm sure she and the baby will both be fine. Have you two decided on a name?

FRIEND – Yes. Faith.

JONES – (To MALCOLM) Christ. If he has triplets is he gonna name the other two "Hope" and "Charity"?

MALCOLM – Shh.

JONES – What? It's a silent movie ain't it, dummy? Sheesh.

POPE – What a wonderfully spiritual sounding name, Edwin. (Considers, after a beat) And if it is a boy?

FRIEND – We have strong reason to believe it to be a girl. (Turning to her) I want to thank you, Effie. Without your companionship during this voyage, I don't think I could have endured. You are truly an amazing artist, architect, and friend.

JONES – (Quietly to MALCOLM) Ooh. *Now* I'm likin' this.

MALCOLM – What?

JONES – He's gonna hit on her.

MALCOLM – Are you sure?

JONES – I can hope, can't I?

POPE - (Admitting) Oh, Professor, I do enjoy your company, as well. And we have accomplished so much together. Together we will be able to offer the United States the chance to have a psychic university of its very own.

JONES – (Disappointed) Aw, shit.

FRIEND – (Nervous) It is of the great power of the mind I wish to speak, Theodate.

POPE – You are shaking, Edwin. What has you so troubled?

FRIEND - You heard the Captain last night at dinner. We may be finished here. The Germans intend to get us, and I don't want to die not being able to see my baby girl born.

POPE - "Intend to get us"? Listen to yourself, Edwin. You are a Harvard graduate. You shouldn't be speaking in such a defeatist fashion. Leave that to those upstarts over at Yale.

FRIEND – I can't help it. Remember what Sir Oliver said about Alta Piper? He said she was also supposed to be there to attend the wedding of his daughter.

POPE – I remember. He said her mother didn't want her going.

FRIEND – Right. Her mother was positive that something might happen, but Alta didn't care. Oliver told us that she got as far as New York when all of a sudden, the night before we sailed this wave of unease swept across her. "All night", he said, "A voice called out to her, saying, 'If you get into your berth, you'll never get out.'" Now that feeling of dread is all over this ship. You can feel it. (Admitting) I…I feel it.

POPE – Nonsense. I have also heard such foolish talk. Why, I overheard the maid saying that the chief bedroom steward isn't here because his wife had a premonition that the ship would sink. So, she pleaded with him not to come and he didn't. Stuff and nonsense. We study clairvoyance, Edwin. You know how powerful a weapon the power of suggestion can be. But don't panic, Professor. I had a dream, too.

FRIEND – I remember, the bugler, yes.

POPE - I dreamt I saw the crew, sailors, stewards, cooks all working together, loosening the ship's boats and swinging them clear of the railing. There was a great fog all around. Then, the ship's bugler woke me. When I looked out of my window, there they all were, just as I saw in my dream. So, I am comforted at the thought that we will surely be convoyed. There will be no sinking today, Professor. Don't be a defeatist. (MALCOLM looks up from his camera, frustrated he can't do or say anything)

JONES – What? What's the matter, bud? (MALCOLM says nothing and returns to filming. DAVIES enters and crosses from stage right to stage left calling through the cabin)

DAVIES – Mr. and Mrs. Baldwin. Telegraph message for Mr. and Mrs. Harry Baldwin. (Repeats as he exits)

FRIEND – (Smiling at POPE) Dear lady, I want you to promise me, no matter what, that should I not make it back home, you'll continue our work and try to communicate with me so that I might see my Marjorie and Faith once more. (She begins to protest but he stops her) Promise?

POPE – (Conceding) Very well, I promise. Now, let's stop all this imprudent talk and walk out on the deck. Perhaps they'll play a nice waltz to pass the time. I'm feeling a second wind coming on and I want to dance.

FRIEND – (Standing, gallantly extending his hand to her) Very good, Miss. Shall we?

POPE – Lets. (Both exit off left as MALCOLM sees YVONNE again)

JONES – (Annoyed) God, now I wish the Krauts *would* torpedo us...them two first. (POPE returns and gently puts her hand on MALCOLM's arm)

POPE – She has loved you for years. (Exits)

MALCOLM – What? (Confused) How...?

JONES – Newman, you're killing me, here. Here come the musicians. Keep filming. Maybe they'll play something.

MALCOLM – (Mocking Jones earlier comment) It's a silent movie, ain't it?

JONES – Shush. Film. (MALCOLM returns to filming. THREE MUSICIANS enter from stage left, crossing in front of the camera. TWO carry violin cases)

MUSICIAN # 1 – (In a British accent) They say the musicians went down playing on Titanic when it sank.

MUSICIAN # 2 – (In a British accent) Bollocks, mate. I want to live. If we get blasted, let the tenor go down with the ship singing, then.

MUSICIANS # 1 and # 3 – Aye. (EXIT off right)

JONES – (To MALCOLM) Can this day get any worse? Jeez. (An attractive FEMALE PASSENGER walks by, turns around and winks at JONES) Oooh. I, uh, need to get a drink. See ya. (Exits off right)

MALCOLM – (Calling after JONES) Not much film left, Mr. Jones. (To HIMSELF) This must be all the footage that we couldn't save. I've got to do something, but what? Got to find Yvonne. (LADY ALLAN enters from stage right with her two daughters, ANNA and GWENDOLYN. The girls are wearing white dresses all covered in grey paint stains. She has them by their ears and is quite angry)

LADY ALLAN – (In a French accent) Mon Dieu! I cannot believe you two girls would be so careless! How did you get paint all over your new dresses?

ANNA – (In a French accent) We only wanted to help, Mama.

GWENDOLYN – The sailor was painting one of the lifeboats.

ANNA – We asked if we could help.

GWENDOLYN – But he said "I hardly think this is a job for girls." Hmmph!

ANNA – So, I borrowed the rag he was using...

LADY ALLAN – Stole the rag...

ANNA – Oui, I took the rag he was using and began painting the boat.

LADY ALLAN – And the deck and yourselves. Look at you! The man must have been furious.

GWENDOLYN – Oui, Mama.

LADY ALLAN – What happened next?

ANNA - He heard his boss approaching. The sailor he leaped over the side of the boat down onto a lower deck. I dropped the rag.

GWENDOLYN – We ran.

LADY ALLAN – Mon Dieu! The sooner we get back to Canada the sooner I shall make your lives miserable. (Exits off left with the girls, GWENDOLYN waving to MALCOLM before she exits. MALCOLM waves back then returns to shooting the camera as ROWLAND enters the party stage right with DOROTHY BRAITHWAITE)

DOROTHY – (In a French accent, calling after LADY ALLAN) Lady Allan! Oh, Lady Allan! Blast. I wanted to say I would meet her for lunch. Oh, well. She seems to have other things on her mind right now. (ROWLAND smiles and laughs) I do so want to thank you again for the wonderful party on boat the other day, Mr. Rowland. I cannot believe it was put together so quickly.

ROWLAND –You are quite welcome Miss Braithwaite. I only wish your journey to London were as happy an occasion.

DOROTHY – Oui, my sisters are in a great deal of pain, I'm afraid.

ROWLAND – Uncanny, to lose both husbands on the same day.

DOROTHY – I'll be glad when this awful business is over and done with. I do so want to get there to comfort them.

ROWLAND – (Reassuring) We shall be there soon, Miss...

DOROTHY – S'il vous plaît. Call me Dorothy.

ROWLAND – (Smiling at her) Dorothy. What a lovely name.

DOROTHY – (Smiling back at ROWLAND. She obviously finds him attractive) Merci.

SCHWIEGER – (Offstage, in a British accent) It is only sad that bad things come in threes.

ROWLAND – What was that, Reverend Toner? (SCHWIEGER enters from stage right. He is now dressed as a proper English parson. MALCOLM recognizes him immediately and stops filming)

SCHWIEGER – I was just saying there is a tragic superstition that death is supposed to happen in cycles of three. I hope that is not true in your case, my dear Miss Braithwaite.

DOROTHY – I hope so, too, Reverend. I would hate to even think of the loss of another loved one.

SCHWIEGER – (Knowing, sadly) Aye.

MALCOLM - Schwieger! (JONES returns with YVONNE and the FEMALE PASSENGER. He has obviously been having a good time but YVONNE does not wish to be with either of them)

JONES – (To MALCOLM) What the hell, dummy? Why did you stop filming?

ROWLAND – (Turns to MALCOLM) Is there a problem, Mr. Newman?

MALCOLM – (Tries to speak but cannot, then offers) No, sir. (To JONES) Uh, need another reel. This one's almost full. (To ROWLAND) I was wondering if…the Reverend…could spare a moment?

SCHWIEGER – Certainly, my son.

ROWLAND – (Politely extending his arm to DOROTHY) May I escort you to your table, Dorothy? (DOROTHY smiles, takes ROWLAND by the arm and together they exit off left. JONES, the FEMALE PASSENGER and YVONNE follow them out, with YVONNE throwing MALCOLM a curious look before she goes. She is obviously attracted to him. SCHWIEGER crosses to MALCOLM)

MALCOLM – Yvonne, I…(Sees that she is gone) Dammit.

SCHWIEGER – (In his German accent again) I know your frustration, Herr Newman.

MALCOLM – (Looking at SCHWIEGER's priestly attire) So, it is you. What's this outfit supposed to be, Schwieger? Sarcasm?

SCHWIEGER – Here I am the Reverend Toner. I am a survivor of the Titanic and the Empress of Ireland.

MALCOLM – Your ability to avoid disasters astounds me.

SCHWIEGER – (Shaking his head) Avoid? Everyone has a destiny, Herr Newman. You are here because you are supposed to be here…as am I.

MALCOLM – Just who the hell are you, "Reverend"? Tell me why I can't speak. Every time I want to, nothing comes out. I can't even get close to Yvonne. I tried to get the shot of her speaking to me but she ran away.

SCHWIEGER – It is as I said. Neither you nor I can warn anybody about the attack.

MALCOLM – This is history and I get that, but how can I just watch things knowing I can't change it? And shouldn't I still be able to get Yvonne to record and send her message to me? Isn't *that* part of history, too?

SCHWIEGER – Yes, and it will happen when the…time is appropriate. (LILLIAN silently chases VANDERBILT into the room. BOTH are in varied states of disrobing. YVONNE returns with JONES, POPE and FRIEND)

MALCOLM – Appropriate? That torpedo is about to strike at any moment, for Christ's sake! How the hell can I not tell these people that they ALL died here? (Turns to see YVONNE, POPE, JONES, FRIEND, LILLIAN and VANDERBILT, all with stunned expressions on their face) Shit.

SCHWIEGER – (Just as LIGHTS DIM) Now, this presents a problem.

Blackout

End of Act One

ACT TWO

Act 2, Scene 1 - RMS Lusitania - Vanderbilt Cabin – Moments Later

(There is a loud cacophony of voices ad libbing concern as LIGHTS UP and the scene continues virtually where it left off at the end of Act 1. YVONNE, POPE and FRIEND are off stage right. JONES, LILLIAN and VANDERBILT are next to MALCOLM. SCHWIEGER has already exited)

MALCOLM –Please, everybody, please!

YVONNE – Malcolm, what're ye sayin'?

LILLIAN – (To MALCOLM) How do you know we're all gonna die? (To YVONNE) Hey! That's my fuckin' confession dress!

JONES – (Pointing at the camera) We can't lose that film!

YVONNE – The film? Is that all ye care about, now? What about every man, woman and child on board?

JONES – Let 'em get their own cameras. (Ad lib arguing continues)

VANDERBILT – Where did the priest go?

MALCOLM –Hold on a second! I want to tell you everything I know, believe me. But every time I start, I sort of…well, I get "stuck".

JONES – What? You mean like constipation?

MALCOLM – No, it's more like something putting a hand over my mouth, keeping me from telling you.

YVONNE - The priest. Does he have something to do with all of this?

MALCOLM – (Unable to verbally confirm) I'm sorry.

VANDERBILT – (Accusing) You mean you won't speak. What are you? Some sort of German spy?

YVONNE – (Defending MALCOLM) I don't believe he is refusin' to answer, Mr. Vanderbilt.

POPE – (Chiming in) It's that he can't answer. (To MALCOLM) That's it, isn't it?

LILLIAN – (To MALCOLM) But you said we all died. Past tense. Like you knew.

MALCOLM – I can't explain. I'm sorry. I wish I could.

JONES – (Pulling LILLIAN aside) Hey! Wait a sec, Lil. Think about it. Titanic and Empress of Ireland. There has never been any filming of those wrecks. If it's true and the ship does get racked by the Krauts, we got film of it which could be worth thousands, maybe even millions someday.

LILLIAN – (Sarcastic) But we gotta survive first, don't we, Ernie?

JONES – There's a lot of empty lifeboats. We grab what we need from the cabin and take off. Whaddaya say? (LILLIAN nods)

POPE – (Realizing) He did know.

FRIEND – What? But how is that possible, Miss Pope?

POPE – Simple. He has the gift. (Indicating YVONNE) As does she. (YVONNE looks guilty. JONES gestures to LILLIAN to grab the camera and exit the room)

MALCOLM – I don't have any…(Considers, then crosses to YVONNE) Is that true? Did you know about today? Is that why you sent me the message?

YVONNE – I sent no message.

MALCOLM – But you did. I got one. (Considers again) Wait. Maybe… (JONES and LILLIAN are gone)

POPE – Maybe she must do so now?

MALCOLM – Sure, that's it. But this wasn't the room.

YVONNE – What are ye both sayin'? 'Tis madness.

MALCOLM – (Remembering) Yvonne, tell me about Belvoir Forest.

VANDERBILT – (Annoyed) Now? Christ!

MALCOLM – (To YVONNE, urging) Please.

YVONNE – (Smiling, curious) Belvoir Forest? You know it? What about…?

MALCOLM – You have a favorite place there, right? A tree?

YVONNE – My dear God. How can ye know this?

MALCOLM – Trust me, please? Just tell me. It means something to you, doesn't it? Something special?

YVONNE – (Admitting, recollecting) Aye. It's the oldest, greenest, most beautiful tree I think in all of Ireland. As kids we used to climb it every day. Then, my parents died and I was sent away to different places. But even now it is the happiest memory I think I have of my childhood. Malcolm…how could ye know that? Who are ye?

MALCOLM – I'm a man who has loved you from thousands miles away and a hundred years from now. (To POPE) Ma'am, you know something about all this, don't you?

FRIEND – You must tell us, Miss Pope.

POPE – I had a dream. This woman was calling out to you. That's all I know except she wasn't calling from here. It was someplace else. There was a lot of fog. No…not fog. It was…smoke. (Realizing) There was a fire.

FRIEND –The boat? (Realizing) The ship was on fire.

VANDERBILT – Then, that's it. We *will* get hit.

MALCOLM – (Nodding, but still cannot verbally confirm. Speaks to YVONNE) When we met in Jones's cabin, you looked at me as if you knew me. Is that true?

YVONNE – (Admitting) Not by name, but I've spent the last nineteen years dreaming of ye. Usually it would be random, vague impressions. Only in the last few months have the impressions become more… distinct. I never even knew if it was real. All I did know is, just like ye said, I have loved ye in all that time.

FRIEND – Theodate was right. You both have been given these exceptional gifts. If only there were more time, we could further explore them.

MALCOLM – More time? How ironic.

VANDERBILT – We must tell the Captain.

FRIEND – Tell him what?

YVONNE – Yes, the Professor is right. We have no proof. (Looks at MALCOLM) Just feelings.

POPE – (Turns to FRIEND with concern) Edwin. Your wife.

FRIEND – Oh, my God. Yes. (To MALCOLM) Yes! My wife is pregnant. I must return home.

VANDERBILT – As do I, Professor. I have interests…my wife being top of the list.

POPE – I'm sure there is a person for everyone on this ship. (MALCOLM and YVONNE look at one another and smile)

VANDERBILT - Guess we're all in the same "boat" then, eh? (NO ONE laughs) Sorry.

YVONNE - There must be a way to save everybody.

VANDERBILT – (Comes up with an idea) I've got it! Stackhouse.

MALCOLM – What?

VANDERBILT – Commander Stackhouse. A few of us have been speculating he's actually a British agent on a secret mission. He's been a little too obvious, trying to ease the calm by saying things like "Oh, this boat is much too fast to be torpedoed".

POPE – Yes. You're right. At lunch the other day he was telling me that (imitating STACKHOUSE) "there are far too many Americans on board so the Germans wouldn't dare try anything".

VANDERBILT – He's staying in A-34. I'll go speak with him now.

POPE – We'll go with you, Mr. Vanderbilt.

MALCOLM – Why don't we all go?

POPE – No. I believe you and the young lady have some unfinished business to attend to.

MALCOLM – Right. (Looks around the cabin) The camera. The camera's gone.

YVONNE – So are Mr. Jones and Lillian.

MALCOLM – Oh, God. The film. We were almost out of film. Yvonne, let's go.

(LIGHTS DIM. Scene TRANSITIONS to Act 2, Scene 2)

Act 2, Scene 2 - RMS Lusitania – Main Deck Railing – Moments Later

(VANDERBILT, POPE and FRIEND are standing with COMMANDER STACKHOUSE who sips a cup of coffee from a fine China cup)

COMMANDER STACKHOUSE – Torpedo? Stuff and nonsense. You must have had quite a time last night. I see you're all still wearing the same clothes. Must have been quite a party, Vanderbilt. (Laughs)

VANDERBILT – Stackhouse, we know it sounds mad, but we have it on good authority this ship could be hit at any moment. (COWPER runs on from stage right) What is it, Cowper?

COWPER – (Pointing out) Look! Out there! The U-boat!

VANDERBILT – What? I don't see anything.

STACKHOUSE - Don't be an alarmist, young man. The Germans can't get near us.

COWPER – But it's the conning tower. It's right there. We've got to warn the Captain. (Exits)

VANDERBILT – (Looks out) I see it, too. (To STACKHOUSE) Stackhouse, we must convince the Captain to launch the lifeboats now.

STACKHOUSE – Don't be insane, man. There's nothing out there. Don't you think I'd recognize a conning tower if I saw one? It's probably just a flock of seagulls attacking a fish or something.

FRIEND – How can you be so imperceptive, sir?

STACKHOUSE – (Insulted) Professor, we couldn't be safer. The watches have been doubled, the men are looking out for the U-boat, and right from here you could see the periscope a mile away.

POPE – Commander, you must trust us. We are in imminent danger.

STACKHOUSE – (Chuckling) "Imminent danger"? My good woman, I know you believe in the power of the mind, and all, but really such flight of fancy must be taken with a grain of salt. The Lusitania could not possibly be…

(Before he can finish there is a loud sound of two almost simultaneous explosions. ALL lean to one side followed by a momentary BLACKOUT. There are multiple sounds of crashing waves of water and debris, crashing glass and people screaming. SCHWIEGER is isolated stage right out of the darkness. He speaks to the audience with cold dread. The following is from the actual log entry made by the German U-boat commander)

SCHWIEGER – It was a clear bow shot. Angle of intersection 90 degrees. Shot struck starboard side close behind the bridge. An extraordinary heavy detonation followed, with a very large cloud of smoke, far above the front funnel. A second explosion must have followed that of the torpedo, boiler or coal or powder, perhaps? The superstructure above the point of impact and the bridge were torn apart. Fire broke out and light smoke veiled the high bridge. The ship stopped immediately and quickly listed sharply to starboard, sinking deeper by the head at the same time. (SCHWIEGER exits into darkness. At LIGHTS UP the deck and railing are smashed with only half of the set remaining standing. There is smoke. PROFESSOR FRIEND is missing. MISS POPE, VANDERBILT and STACKHOUSE are all on the ground, disheveled in appearance now. LADY ALLEN rushes past from stage right as GERDA runs in from stage left. Both are looking beaten, frazzled and frantic)

LADY ALLEN – Anna? Gwendolyn? Girls? Where are you? (Exits off left)

GERDA – John? Please God, not John. John? John! (DAVIES comes up with SARAH LUND and BOTH assist GERDA)

DAVIES – This way, mum. Lifeboats are this way. Come along everyone! No delays. Hurry! (Exits off right with GERDA and LUND as VANDERBILT and STACKHOUSE lift POPE up to her feet)

GERDA - (As she's being led out) John! Answer me! John!

VANDERBILT – (To STACKHOUSE) You were saying, Commander?

STACKHOUSE – (Stunned) It... can't be.

VANDERBILT – Has Titanic taught you nothing, you stupid old fool?

POPE – (Looking for FRIEND) Edwin? (Concerned) Edwin? (Looks over to one side and sees FRIEND dead in the water) Oh, my God. No. Edwin. (Turns away in horror. DENYER enters from far right and comes up to VANDERBILT. He, too, is disheveled in appearance from the explosion)

DENYER – (Out of breath) Mr. Vanderbilt. Cabins smashed, sir. Blown apart. I found Mr. Williamson and Miss Baker. Both dead.

VANDERBILT – Sorenson?

DENYER – Went over the side sir...still carrying his poker hand.

VANDERBILT – Must have had that winning hand, then.

DENYER - There are people dead all over the ship. The lifeboats, sir. Most of 'em are smashed. Intact maybe five or six at the most. (LIGHTS momentarily DIM. SCHWIEGER is isolated out of the darkness again far downstage right. He recites from memory another passage from the U-boat captain's log)

SCHWIEGER – (Emotionless) Great confusion arose on the ship; some of the boats were swung clear and lowered into the water. Many people must have lost their heads. Several boats loaded with people rushed downward, struck the water bow or stern first and filled at once. On the port side, because of the sloping position, fewer boats were swung clear than on the starboard side. (Becoming more emotional) The ship blew off steam. At the bow the name "Lusitania" in golden letters was visible. (SCHWIEGER once again exits into the darkness as LIGHTS UP on the scene once more)

VANDERBILT – (Realizing) There were two explosions.

DENYER – What, sir?

VANDERBILT – Just now there were two explosions. (Grabbing STACKHOUSE by the lapels) There were TWO explosions, but only one torpedo. What do you have on board, Stackhouse?

STACKHOUSE – What?

VANDERBILT – (Screaming) What are we carrying? What's in the cargo hold?

STACKHOUSE – (Admitting) Munitions. This is an auxiliary war ship. We were sworn to secrecy.

VANDERBILT – You damned fools. You placed all these women and children in danger? And you call me insane? You arrogant bastard. (Lets go of STACKHOUSE. Turns to DENYER) Denyer. We must act fast. We will help get the women and kids to the lifeboats, quick as we can.

DENYER – Right, sir. (DENYER exits off left. VANDERBILT sees POPE clinging to what's left of the railing)

VANDERBILT - Come along, Miss Pope. (POPE doesn't move. VANDERBILT pulls her away from the railing) Please hurry. (STACKHOUSE is also in a daze) Stackhouse?

STACKHOUSE – You go ahead. I'll be along in a moment. Vanderbilt? (VANDERBILT turns back to him) Save as many as you can. (VANDERBILT nods then together him and POPE exit off left. STACKHOUSE takes out a pen and paper and scribbles furiously. ROWLAND enters from far right, carrying the damp, limp, bloodied body of DOROTHY BRAITHWAITE. He places her to the ground and begins crying. STACKHOUSE looks at and reads aloud what he has written) "Let mercy be our boast, and shame our only fear". (He puts the paper in his pocket and turns to ROWLAND) Rowland.

ROWLAND – (Defeated, sad) I pulled her from the water, but she was already lost.

STACKHOUSE – (Lifting ROWLAND to his feet) Come along, man. There's nothing you can do for her now. We'll grieve later. Right now we must try to save the women and children. Lord, forgive us. What have we done? (LIGHTS DIM. Scene TRANSITIONS to Act 2, Scene 3)

Act 2, Scene 3 - RMS Lusitania - Ernest Jones Cabin – Moments Later

(In darkness there again are multiple sounds of crashing waves of water and debris, crashing glass and people screaming. As LIGHTS UP we are back in JONES's cabin. The room is in complete disarray with smoke filling the cabin. There is the sound of flame indicating then cabin is burning. The bodies of LILLIAN and JONES are on the floor. MALCOLM and YVONNE enter from the entrance door)

YVONNE – Oh, my God! Lillian!

MALCOLM – Don't bother. She and Jones are both dead. (Feeling the boat start to lean) She's starting to list. She'll go under any moment. (Picks up YVONNE who is at LILLIAN's body) Yvonne! We need to find the camera.

YVONNE – (Looking by the bed, seeing that the camera is knocked over) There! Over by the bed!

MALCOLM – Fine. (Picks it up) It's undamaged. Film is still in there. They didn't get a chance to pack it up yet. All right. Give me two seconds then start speaking.

YVONNE – I'm not sure I can. I mean, Lillian…

MALCOLM – It's going. (YVONNE doesn't speak, moves away from the camera line of shot) Yvonne, don't give up now. I came here because you called out to me. If you don't do this…maybe…

YVONNE – But you're here, now, Malcolm. We have so little time. We can't be selfish. We need to save as many as we can. (MALCOLM relents. They hug, then kiss. Then YVONNE says) Please. Let's just go. I don't want to die here.

MALCOLM – You won't. I promise. (As the ship lists more) Okay. Fine. I'll…

YVONNE – Oh, Miss Pope. We need to get her, as well.

MALCOLM –We don't know. She might be dead already.

YVONNE – She's not. I can feel it. She's alive, Malcolm. Go. Run. I'll be right behind you. I promise. (MALCOLM exits, turning back one time to YVONNE then heads out. YVONNE grabs a couple of items then begins to leave the cabin when she stops, turns back to see SCHWIEGER at the cabin entrance) It's you. Have ye come to kill me, as well, then? Come to finish the job? (SCHWIEGER says nothing. He merely goes to the back of the camera and starts cranking it. YVONNE, hesitant at first, approaches and speaks into the camera) Malcolm, please save me! Malcolm help! (SCHWIEGER stops the camera. Saying nothing, he takes the film off the tripod and hands it to YVONNE. Hearing another explosion, she grabs the film, puts it into a container then exits as the flames and smoke get worse. SCHWIEGER merely stands there for a moment, then sits on the sofa as LIGHTS DIM. The horrific sounds of waves crashing and people screaming gets worse as the Lusitania sinks. Scene TRANSITIONS to Act 2, Scene 4)

SCHWIEGER – (Isolated in darkness) There was a mass of foam and then flat calm where Lusitania used to be. In the distance, a number of life-boats were moving. Nothing more was to be seen of the Lusitania, the wreck fourteen nautical miles from the Old Head of Kinsale lighthouse. (LIGHTS DIM)

Act 2, Scene 4 - The Home of Ethel McShane-Bryce – Sunday morning

(At LIGHTS UP, we are back at the home of Ethel McShane-Bryce. It is the same morning of MALCOLM's "departure". DOUG comes down the stairs in a bathrobe. JANICE follows him slowly, also in a bathrobe)

JANICE – Doug? How are ye holding up?

DOUG – Stunned. Just can't believe it. Gone. Just like that.

JANICE – I know. 'Tis said. I feel like I just lost family and yet we only just met.

DOUG – (Shaking his head) I just can't believe Malcolm's gone. I thought he had been managing it so well these last few years.

JANICE – As a caregiver I have seen brain tumors attack a person very quickly. At least he died in his sleep. The doctor's will be over to collect his body in a few minutes. Is there anyone we can call? I know ye said he didn't have a wife. Any parents? Children?

DOUG - (Moving over to his lap top, puts on latex gloves) There's gonna be a lot more work done on this film footage back in New York, but I know he'd want me to finish up our work here first. I just want to take one last look before I change and pack up to bring him…(Can't finish the sentence. Pulls the film out of the canister and takes a look at it, closely. He is perturbed by something)

JANICE – What is it?

DOUG – (Handling the film) The film. It's clear.

JANICE – I don't understand.

DOUG – I mean it's absolutely clear. There's nothing on it.

JANICE – (Looking at the film while he holds it) What happened, then?

DOUG – I don't know. If it was the air it would have corroded or I'd see smudges along the inline. This is clear, as if nothing was ever shot. Oh, Mac. I'm so sorry. I let you down.

JANICE – Don't say that. (Remembering) You saved it on your flashdrive, didn't ye?

DOUG – My flashdrive. Right. (Opens up his lap top and looks for it. As he does, ETHEL appears at the top of the stairs) It's gone. All of it. Gone. Like it never existed.

JANICE – I'm sorry. Ye didn't answer my question before. Did he have any children?

ETHEL – Aye, he did, child. (DOUG and JANICE turn to see ETHEL on the stairs. Still walking with a cane, she is feeling much better, dressed up in her Sunday best) One daughter, a twin with a brother who passed away in 1997. Together those two children had a combined total of eight grandkids and over thirty great grandchildren.

JANICE – (Laughing) Great grandma, that's you ye're thinkin' of.

ETHEL – Aye, and I know what I'm sayin' luv.

JANICE – What? Do ye mean to say that Malcolm was a relative?

DOUG – (Muttering to JANICE) I think she's lost it, kid.

ETHEL – (ETHEL hands JANICE a piece of paper) Malcolm, my dear, was the beginning. (Heading to the front door)

JANICE – What's this? And just where do ye think ye're goin'?

ETHEL – I'm wearin' my Sunday best. I'm off to church to confess…(Smiles) and to give thanks. (Exits)

DOUG – This is nuts. My best friend is dead and now she's the picture of health? I mean, who is she? Vampira? God, my nerves are shot. I need a drink. Anything in the house?

JANICE – Nay, but the bar should be openin' soon. After they come for Malcolm, do ye want to head over there? We can drink a toast to him.

DOUG – Sure. I better get cleaned up. (The TWO head up the stairs when he turns to her and says) By the way, the sex last night was great.

JANICE – Thank ye. Ye'r not so bad yerself. (LIGHTS FADE. Transition to Act 2, Scene 5)

Act 2, Scene 5 - Small Bar - Dover, England – Later Same Day

(LIGHTS UP on the bar. DOUG and JANICE are seated as they were for Act 1, Scene 1. Again TWO OLD MARINERS are seated to the table next to them. The BARMAID comes up and speaks to DOUG)

BARMAID – Ah! Back again, are we?

DOUG – (Looking around) My God. We left here three days ago and it looks like we never left. (To the BARMAID) Two ales, please. No. Make it four. We're toasting someone.

BARMAID – Aye. Will yer friend be joinin' ya, again?

DOUG – (Melancholy) No. No, he won't.

BARMAID – (Curious) Aye. On the way. (Exits)

DOUG – (Stands up, looking around the room, calls out) Hey! Listen up!

JANICE – Jesus! What're doin', Doug?

DOUG - Anybody here old enough to remember the sinking of Lusitania?

MARINER # 1 – (Responding) Aye. My grandfather was first mate on it. What is it you want to know?

DOUG – Let me buy you a beer, old timer. (THE TWO MARINERS joins DOUG and JANICE) I know I could probably Google this...

MARINER # 1 – What's a "Google"...?

DOUG – Never mind. But I want to hear it from a human being. I know it was torpedoed, but how much do you remember about the sinking?

MARINER # 1 – Mostly what I learned from others. It had nineteen hundred sixty passengers and only seven hundred sixty or so survived.

JANICE – Survived? Are ye sure?

MARINER # 1 – Aye.

DOUG – What?

JANICE – That paper me great grandmother gave to me, Doug. I thought it was just her scribbling nonsense, but ye better read it.

DOUG – (Taking the letter and reading it aloud) "As I write this to my future children, I am on a lifeboat off the coast of Ireland having just survived Lusitania. Today I met Yvonne, your mother, and the woman I will love till the end of my days, for whatever time we might share. Doug, if you are reading this…holy shit… in my time it was widely known that all had perished on Lusitania. I tried to change that, but Lusitania sunk anyway. Schwieger was right. I couldn't change history. But if we survived, maybe a few others did, too." The rest of its decayed, illegible. (To JANICE, incredulous) Can't be. This was written a hundred years ago. I mean, look at the paper.

JANICE – I know. But did ye see what he wrote? In his time, *all* had perished on Lusitania.

DOUG – What? You saying they didn't? Gotta remember (pointing to himself) not a history buff.

JANICE – If ye had asked me yesterday, I would have said all of 'em died. But today, like this man said, it was seven hundred sixty or so what survived. Doug, maybe…maybe Malcolm *did* change history.

DOUG – Now hold it, hold it, hold it. Janice. You can't be serious. He died. He died this morning. (Looks again at the paper, considering the possibility) And, even if I did believe it, who was this Schwieger, anyway?

MARINER # 2 – (Slowly recognizing the name) "Schwieger"? The Baby Killer? (Stands, face becomes pale as if he has seen a ghost) No.

DOUG – What? What is it? You heard of this guy?

MARINER # 2 – Schwieger…was the U-boat captain that sunk Lusitania. Some said he felt so guilty that he could not fire a second torpedo into the crushing crowd of humanity trying to save their lives.

MARINER # 1 –(To MARINER # 2) Aye, but it didn't stop him from killin' again, now did it? (To DOUG) That bastard sunk the Hesperian, another passenger liner, not four months later after the world condemned him for Lusitania.

MARINER # 2 – And that ship was carryin' the body of a Lusitania victim headed home for burial, making them twice a victim of Schwieger…and of Lusitania.

MARINER # 1 – British called him the "Baby Killer" because of all the children and pregnant women on board these ships. Schwieger was responsible for the sinkin' of forty-nine ships before justice caught up with him. He was killed in the war couple years later.

MARINER # 2 – Fittin' punishment, if you ask me. His body forever entombed in a submarine. His spirit havin' to atone for all the lives he took. (The BARMAID brings over the drinks and places them down)

DOUG – Thanks. Hey. You ever hear the name Schwieger?

BARMAID – Nope. Can't say that I have, luv. Sorry. (To the MARINERS) Drink up, laddies.

MARINER # 1 – Aye. (The TWO MARINERS pick up their drinks and leave)

DOUG – (Calling out after the TWO MARINERS) I was actually gonna drink those…no?...okay. (To JANICE) A ghost? Really? Come on.

JANICE – Well, Ethel used to tell me of this old spirit medium her mother knew in New York.

DOUG – Yeah?

JANICE – She said for years she tried to reach the spirit of somebody she knew had perished on a doomed ship. Maybe this was like that. A spirit desperately needing to reach out to one of us…to Malcolm.

DOUG – Even if I bought into any of this, which I don't, I mean, why? The man killed thousands upon thousands of people when he was alive. If Schwieger was that malevolent, why would he now send Malcolm to go save Yvonne? And why would he even care enough to let Malcolm and Lillian live?

JANICE – I don't know. Penitence, perhaps? Some believe that no soul is allowed into Heaven until there has been atonement for the past. Maybe Schwieger cannot achieve his eternal rest until he rights all the wrongs he caused to humanity.

DOUG – That could take…

JANICE – An eternity. Aye. That it might. That it might. (Holding up a her mug) To Malcolm? (They drink their beers as LIGHTS DIM)

DAVIES – (Emerging from the darkness stage left) Boatswain John Davies managed to get five out of the six lifeboats ready within fifteen minutes, savin' lives before goin' down with the ship. (CAPTAIN TURNER emerges from the darkness stage left and stands next to DAVIES)

CAPTAIN TURNER – Captain Turner miraculously survived the Lusitania sinking, being rescued from the water. He thought he was last man off, but while in the water, he saw a multitude of passengers and crew perish horribly as Lusitania exploded and sunk. (ROWLAND emerges from the darkness stage left to stand by TURNER and DAVIES)

ROWLAND - Many sought to blame Turner for the loss, including the Lord of Admiralty Winston Churchill, but Turner was exonerated by both the Mersey Inquiry and Mayer hearings. In 1916 he was on board another ship that got torpedoed and once again survived. From then on the only thing he captained was a desk. (ROWLAND and DAVIES exit into the darkness once more)

TURNER - After he divorced his first wife Turner married his maid…his beloved…Mabel. (Exiting into darkness once more)

LADY ALLAN – (Emerging from the darkness stage right) Lady Allan would never see her daughters alive again. Out of the one hundred and twenty-four children aboard, they were two out of ninety-four that perished, including thirty-one out of thirty-five infants. One pregnant woman gave birth while in the waters floating outside of Lusitania. Both she and the baby perished. (ERNEST COWPER emerges from the darkness stage right and stands by LADY ALLAN's side)

ERNEST COWPER – Ernest Cowper managed to save a little six year-old girl whose entire family perished aboard Lusitania. They remained in touch until his death in 1933. (VANDERBILT and DENYER emerge from the darkness stage right and join COWPER and LADY ALLAN)

VANDERBILT – Merely speak the name "Vanderbilt" and still, to this day, almost mythic images of greed, self indulgence and debauchery may be conjured in one's mind. But for all of this and perhaps more, Alfred Vanderbilt, in the end, saved many lives.

DENYER – At Vanderbilt's behest, Denyer collected as many children as he could find. He would hand them off to Vanderbilt who would then run the children, two at a time, to nearby lifeboats.

VANDERBILT – Two men, purportedly at different stations in life, working together and paying the ultimate sacrifice so that others from all walks of life would live. (Shaking DENYER's hand) I still wish I had learned to swim. (The TWO MEN smile as ALL exit into the darkness once more)

SARAH LUND – (Emerging from the darkness stage left) Sarah was hospitalized in Ireland. Both her husband and her father perished. The woman in the institution, however, turned out not to be her mother. William and Charles had died in a quest that had been futile from the start. But at least Sarah knew that her father and mother were finally reunited. (GERDA emerges from the darkness stage left and stands next to LUND)

GERDA - Amid all the death and chaos, stumbling among destruction and confusion, Gerda managed to find John and the two made it to the lifeboats. They were married one week later. However...

JOHN – (Emerging from the darkness stage left) However, a happy ending was not to be, for Gerda had witnessed too much pain and suffering aboard the Lusitania. She went insane. John had her committed until her death in 1961, forty-six years after Lusitania. (Gently taking GERDA's hand both exit into the darkness once more with LUND)

POPE - (Emerging from the darkness stage right) Edwin, who truly died a hero while trying to save another, never got to meet his daughter, Faith. The Professor's body was never recovered. For years Miss Pope would hold séances where it is rumored she saw the spirit of Edwin. Edwin, in death, was reportedly angered over the "dastardly deed" that ended his life, purportedly laying a curse on those responsible. (Exiting into the darkness once more)

SCHWIEGER – (Slowly emerging from darkness to stage center. He is a frantic, tortured soul. He screams to the sky) Is it enough? How about now? Is it enough? How many more? How many more times? (Waits for a response, then after a beat) Fine. One more, then. One more. (LIGHTS DIM as he cries into the darkness amid the sounds of waves crashing against the shore and a ship's steam whistle off in the distance is heard)

Blackout

The End

www.ingramcontent.com/pod-product-compliance
Lightning Source LLC
Chambersburg PA
CBHW070715180526
45167CB00004B/1477